REALLY? REALLY! You better believe it!

The Economist's Bible

AUTHOR

Dwight M. Brose

Copyright applied for
2013

TABLE OF CONTENTS - Page 199

INTRODUCTION - Page 3

**The basic content of this book begins on page 12**

# INTRODUCTION

GOVERNMENT INTERVENTION CAUSES ECONOMIC SLUMPS TO BECOME RECESSIONS AND DEPRESSIONS  Page 78

BANKRUPTCY AND COMPETITION ARE THE BEST REGULATIONS ANY ECONOMY COULD EVER HAVE  Page 86

NO ONE WOULD EVER HAVE TO WORK FOR A LIVING AGAIN. Page 51

SUGAR CAUSES CANCER!  YES IT DOES!  Check it out.  What have you got to lose?  Page 121

Do you know why animals of the wild do not need a trillion dollar a year medical system?  Because they go by natures rules.  Who said that people are smarter than animals? - Page 121

COMPASSION, KINDNESS, NURTURING?  We need more of Father Nature's truth, reality and tough love.  Page 35

**If everyone is kind and nurturing but everyone starts starving and freezing because no one is producing wealth, where is the compassion in that?  No one is entitled to a free ride.  But when Government destroys opportunity, Government is responsible for the hardship. - Page 36**

IS HEALTH CARE A BASIC RIGHT?  Page 39

I DON'T BELIEVE THE MEMBERS OF THE SUPREME COURT ARE DOING THEIR JOB AS OUR FOREFATHERS HAD INTENDED.  Obamacare - Page 41

WHAT SHOULD POLITICIANS AND REGULATORS DO TO STIMULATE A WEAK ECONOMY? NOTHING!  STAY OUT OF THE WAY! Page  55

"PRIVATE INVESTMENT DOESN'T WORK, IT NEVER DID!" Mr. Obama actually said that, Page 25

The reason why Big Government doesn't work is because the only money Government has is "other people's money" and the "other people" get tired of being the sucker and stop creating the wealth. That is why Keynesians constantly try to create money out of nothing. That is why Socialism is always desperate.

LOW INTEREST RATES - HIGH UNEMPLOYMENT - Page 75

GOVERNMENT INTERVENTION CAUSES ECONOMIC SLUMPS TO BECOME RECESSIONS AND DEPRESSIONS. - Page 78

WHAT HAPPENED TO CONFIDENCE? - Page 73

THE CAUSE OF THE PROBLEM (destruction of the dollar) Page 53

**Mr. Bernanke might be doing us a favor by destroying the dollar faster with his extreme low interest rates and QE3. Because the sooner the US economy hits bottom, the sooner the economy can start to recover. No one wants the economy to continue weakening for ever as in Europe and Japan.**

THE VALUE OF A CURRENCY IS EXTREMELY MISUNDERSTOOD. -Page - 54

**The dollar might not be anchored to gold anymore, but gold is anchored to the dollar. When the value of the dollar goes down the price of gold goes up.**

In a recession or depression or any other form of weak economy the various Governments should cut taxes and reduce the regulations and restrictions to the point that it would be easier to start up a business than it would be to get a job. This would be much simpler, faster, more successful, more direct, more fair to the tax payers and more efficient than using the method Keynes suggested, having Government increase spending. Plus, it would bring back the free market and create jobs.

RISK

Risk is the oil that lubes the capitalist system. Risk should never be regulated, insured or restricted. But the risk taker should be the only one that pays the consequences when risk goes wrong. - Page 73

CAPITALISM LOVES MONOPOLIES BUT MONOPOLIES ARE NOT FREE MARKET. Markets cannot be rational , efficient and self regulating unless they are free markets, free of monopolies, excessive regulations and open to fair competition. - Page 113

COMPETITION IS THE ONLY WAY TO KEEP CAPITALISM HONEST Monopolies destroy that competition.
Page 85

SMALL BUSINESS HAS BEEN BOUGHT OUT BY BIG BUSINESS AND REGULATED TO DEATH BY BIG GOVERNMENT. THAT IS WHAT HAS DESTROYED THE MIDDLE CLASS. - Page 62

SOME PEOPLE HATE THE OPPOSITE SEX

Some people, as they grow older, develop a hatred for the opposite sex. Anyone who develops a hatred for the opposite sex should never find him or herself raising a child of that opposite sex that they hate. That child will grow up to hate society. That is where the young people who become violent and destructive to themselves and other people come from. -      Page 37

"RULE OF LAW" MEANS NOTHING

Rules and laws are merely tools. Rules and laws can be good or bad, depending on the goals and intelligence of the creator or creators of those rules and laws. Before rules and laws are established they should be extensively debated and always have a sunset clause. When rules and laws are engraved in stone, they accumulate endlessly until they imprison a society. Freedom means freedom from excessive rules and laws. Ever heard of the Mayflower? - Page 42

THE WORLD DOES NOT OWE ANYONE A LIVING - Page 34

Everyone has to be someplace. And they have just as much a right to be in this world as you or I, but THE WORLD DOES NOT

5

OWE ANYONE A LIVING. Each individual must work for his or her own survival. If politicians could only understand this and reduce regulations and taxes and give the people the opportunity to help themselves, the economy would boom. There would be less poverty, homelessness, joblessness. Less need for welfare, unemployment compensation and subsidies. And less Socialism.

The wife does not "belong" to the husband. The husband does not "belong" to the wife. Everyone has the right to be an individual. Marriage does not change that right.

EVERY ONE HAS THE RIGHT TO BE STUPID NOW AND THEN, AS LONG AS THEY HAVE THE ABILITY TO WISE UP. But some types of stupidity seem unable to wise up. Bullying is an example of stupidity, harassment is an example of stupidity, dictatorship is an example of stupidity, authoritarianism is an example of stupidity.

If Keynesians believe they can print all the money they need to get themselves out of trouble, why do they even bother to collect taxes? Why don't they just print all the money the Government needs and let the people keep their money? The reason why the Government has to collect taxes is because the Government has no choice. Money must be backed up by real wealth created by wealth producers. Government cannot just print money at its convenience without destroying the currency and the economy. The Keynesians are wrong. Page 51

IMMIGRATION

Immigrants come to the US because they think the US is still the land of opportunity. And the US would still be the land of opportunity if the Government would get out of the way.

If the eleven million immigrants were allowed to work they would create much more wealth for the economy than all the forty seven million people on food stamps do.

How about letting the eleven million immigrants stay and work and sending eleven million people on food stamps to Mexico in their place. Then the US workers who are working would not have to pay for all those food stamps. And the eleven million immigrants would help pay for the rest of the food stamps.

Inflation of any amount destroys the value of the medium of exchange, the country's currency. In 1972 an ounce of gold cost $32. Today, June 2011, one ounce of gold costs over $1500. That means one dollar today is worth only two percent of what it was worth 38 years ago. In other words a dollar today is worth less than two cents compared to 38 years ago. THAT IS INFLATION! Thank you US economists and politicians. Page 19

A big problem in the European Union is that Northern Europe is creating the wealth and Southern Europe is spending it. Someone is going to get tired of being the sucker. Sooner or later reality is going to drag the Europeans, kicking and screaming, out of their dream world and into the real world. It's the "vision thing". But as reality starts kicking more butts, the vision thing becomes more clear. There seems to be nothing more educational than a kick in the butt brought on by the hardship of a poor economy. - Page 68

A PROBLEM WITH DEMOCRACY - Page 23

THE REASON WHY THE ELECTION 2012 WAS SUCH A SURPRISE TO THE REPUBLICANS. Page 41

SOCIALISTS BELIEVE ALL THE MONEY IN THE SOCIETY BELONGS TO THEM - Page 28

SOCIALIST GOVERNMENTS BELIEVE ALL THE MONEY AND THE PEOPLE IN THE SOCIETY BELONGS TO THEM AND THEY HAVE A RIGHT TO DISTRIBUTE THE MONEY AS THEY SEE FIT. Socialism is a Government of "common good". Rules for the good of everyone and the satisfaction of none. In a socialist Democracy, all the rules are made for the "other guy".

LIBERAL
The term liberal was derived from politicians with the attitude that they should solve all society's problems by throwing other people's money at those problems. In other words be liberal with other people's money.

A DEMOCRAT MOTTO;
    "Government is the only thing that we all belong to". That might be true in a monarchy or a dictatorship or in socialism. But in a democracy it is the other way around. "The Government belongs to the people". Page 28

IN THE US, PEOPLE DO NOT BELONG TO THE GOVERNMENT. GOVERNMENT BELONGS TO THE PEOPLE. This very major difference is what is causing the split, the partisanship between the Democrats and the Republicans. Do we want to be sheep or individuals? -Page 28

WHAT IS WEALTH? - Page 15

THE BASICS OF ECONOMICS - How important is currency? - Page 17

INFLATION - Page 55

WORLD INFLATION-CURRENCY WARS - Page 21

SUPPLY AND DEMAND - Pages 45 and 82

THE FED'S MANDATE OF KEEPING INTEREST RATES LOW IN ORDER TO INCREASE EMPLOYMENT IS HAVING THE OPPOSITE EFFECT. Increasing the value of the currency would be the best "jobs program" the Government could possibly produce. Page 105

THE WORLD ECONOMY IS BIGGER THAN JOHN MAYNARD KEYNES
    Europe and the Soviet Union have proven that Socialism doesn't work. The world markets will help make the final decisions. -Page 49

REDUCING VALUE OF CURRENCY DOES NOT INCREASE VALUE OF STOCKS -Page 47

AUSTERITY AND TAX INCREASES-EUROPEAN TROUBLES - Page 67

MONOPOLIES
    TOO BIG TO SUCEED!  WHAT EVER HAPPENED TO THE ANTITRUST AGENCY?  - Page 84

CURRENCY MANIPULATION - U.S. CRITICISM OF OTHER COUNTRIES
    Accusing any country of manipulating its currency is misguided. It is any country's sovereign right to control its currency.  The US manipulates its currency as much as any country, and more than most.
    When the US is manipulating its currency downward in order to help corporations export more, or for any other reason, it is irritating and embarrassing  to hear US regulators and politicians accuse other countries of manipulating their currencies.  The whole world can see what is going on.  So who is the ignorant one?

THE CENTRAL BANKS OF THE WORLD SHOULD STOP, SHOULD DISCONTINUE USING INFLATION TARGETS TO DETERMINE THEIR INTEREST RATES.  CENTRAL BANKS OF THE WORLD SHOULD REPLACE 'INFLATION' AS A TARGET WITH 'CURRENCY VALUE' AS A TARGET - Page 21

INCENTIVE TO BE PRODUCTIVE.  Offer employees a percentage of profits rather than an increase in hourly rate.

ALL SOCIALIST COUNTRIES ARE DESPERATE.  Because sooner or later they always run out of other people's money and the wealth producers get tired of being the sucker.  - Page 44

REDICULOUS REQUESTS BY OPPOSING POLITICIANS AND JOURNALISTS
    Journalists and politicians keep asking their  opponents in a presidential campaign to give details of what their policies will be if elected.  This is such a ridiculous request!  They cannot be expected to know the details.  That is why the elected winner has a multimillion dollar administration, (paid for by the taxpayers), to propose the details.
    The candidate should only be expected to give general theories. The winning candidate's administration gives the elected person  the proposed details, then he or she makes the decisions.  The winning politician is the administrator, not the detailer.

That is why the selection of the newly elected person's administration is so important. The detailed policies come from the administration. If the candidate knew all the answers, he or she would not need a multimillion dollar administration. Even if the elected person had all the answers, the congress would question them and change them.

EXERCISE CAN DEFEND AGAINST ALSHEIMER'S, DEMENTIA, PARKINSONS AND STROKE. YES IT CAN. - Page 117

IN ORDER TO LIVE YOU HAVE TO HAVE HEART, A STRONG HEART. THAT IS THE SECRET TO THE FOUNTAIN OF YOUTH!

I AM WRITING LIKE THERE IS NO TOMORROW. BECAUSE THERE "IS" NO TOMORROW, THANKS TO THE SOCIALISTS. **Socialists believe the whole world belongs to them and everyone in it is their slave. That is wrong. I am not anyone's slave.**

REMEMBER THIS

Many of the theories in this book are derived from nature's rules and laws. They are not my theories, they were around long before I was borne and they will be around long after I am gone. One reason why I am writing this book is because I believe a reminder of nature's rules and laws will help make the world a better place.

Man made rules are all over the place, intruding into everything. Nature's rules are always the same, year after year, generation after generation and nature's rules are the same all over the world.

My brother once said, "How come you are always right?". Well, I am not always right by a long ways but I am right quite often because I go by "Nature's Rules" and Nature's Rules have been around for a long time.

I learned about nature's rules in the State of Montana. I have been all over the State of Montana.

As I write this book, I try not to use big words or uncommon words. I am not trying to impress people with a big vocabulary or with any possible brilliance that I might have. I am trying to communicate with everyone.

I am a western hick. I have never been back East where all the "experts" live.

This is a poem I Wrote:

Montana, Montana, why can't I shake this spell you have on me?

Way down deep inside, I guess this longing will always be.

From the rugged eastern badlands, created recklessly,

Now in this chipped terrain hides captivating mystery.

To the western wild wilderness of fierce and shocking reality.

Bound together by two mighty Rivers that flow finally to the sea.

The last place on  earth where truth is a guarantee.

Even though I can't shake this feeling, that's ok with me.

For though I am far away, Home sweet Home is what you will always be.

REALLY? REALLY! You better believe it!   (By Dwight Brose)


WHICH ARE MORE VALUABLE, THEORIES OR FACTS?
What is "genius"?

Almost everyone has access to the facts if he or she wants to search for them.   There are volumes and volumes of facts on every subject imaginable.  But only a few analytical minds use these facts to create theories that completely transform our society.

Everyone had access to the facts that Bill Gates used to create Microsoft.  Everyone had access to the facts but Thomas Edison came up with the theories that caused tremendous changes in  our society. Everyone had access to the facts that George Soros used for his theories that earned him  billions of dollars in financial investing.  In a free market society, theories are more valuable than facts.

These theories are created by analytical  minds.  All of the trillions of dollars worth of productivity in the world was  brought about by analytical minds.  We would still be dwelling in caves today if the human species did not have the ability to develop analytical minds. These analytical minds came up with the theories that made all this production possible.

But of all the  people in the world only a small percentage has developed the analytical ability to come up with these theories that are worth fortunes.

Just suppose everyone had the potential to develop this type of analytical mind.   Look at all those people who did not develop an analytical mind.  Think of the trillions upon trillions of dollars worth of production and wealth that was not created because these people did not develop an analytical mind.

Suppose that you and I had the potential to develop this type of analytical mind.  Suppose all we had to do was to exercise our brains.

Look at all the muscles Arnold Schwarzenegger developed with exercise. Did Albert Einstein have an Arnold Schwarzenegger type of brain? Did Albert Einstein develop all that brain power or analytical ability through many hours of deep thinking and concentration and possibly a little frustration? Did he develop his analytical ability by doing many hours of rigid calisthenics for the brain?

Thomas Edison said, "Genius is 2% inspiration and 98% perspiration. The 2% is the desire to control your destiny and the 98% part is the rigid calisthenics that exercise the brain. That is exactly what genius is, tremendous analytical ability developed mostly by rigid calisthenics for the brain. The ability to come up with theories that are worth fortunes, the ability to solve problems and be creative.

The brain is like a muscle. Exercise will make it stronger. Thinking is the heavy lifting that develops analytical ability and brain power. It takes challenges, hassles, hazards, hardships, frustrations, stresses, disappointments, mistakes, risks and hard work to develop analytical, problem solving, creative ability.

You have got to admit, life is a lot easier now than it was in the horse and buggy days. In those days everyone was poor because there was much less accumulation of wealth back then. Modern day "easy living" is weakening society's mental capabilities. The poorest members of society will become the strongest members because the hardship will cause them to develop analytical, problem solving, creative ability.

Everyone has the ability to be a genius. Too many times people choose to cruise along at basic animal level without putting the brain into gear. Easy living contributes to laziness and mental weakness.

You don't get analytical ability from reading books, you get it from the school of hard knocks. Solving problems is a very important part of creativity. It appears stuffing the brain with information does not create analytical, problem solving ability.

Don't condemn the odd balls or the nerds or the poor who face the hardship, they are the potential intelligent managers and leaders and geniuses. I'm afraid the "cool", "fly by the seat of your pants" members of society are never going to make the genius roster. Children who are pampered and protected too much by their parents and those who are waiting around for their inheritance are the weak ones. Life is so full of--LIFE if you want to look for it. YOU CAN EXERCISE YOUR BRAIN AND LIVE LONGER! YES YOU CAN!

## THE HUMAN BEING IS THE ONLY ANIMAL THAT CAN DEVELOP ADVANCED ANALYTICAL ABILITY

Karl Marx theorized that one laborer could produce only X amount of wealth, no more no less. He did not allow for any flexibility or variation in the productive ability of various workers. He appeared to believe that humans were like ants or bees. He seemed to have the theory that no one could learn anything. Do socialists have a problem accepting the fact that human abilities can move way beyond "basic animal" abilities?

An ambitious, creative, motivated worker can and will produce many times more wealth than a lazy worker. The incentives in the free market will motivate a worker to produce much more wealth than the unmotivated worker or forced labor in Socialism.

An inventor or entrepreneur with analytical, creative ability can produce fortunes in wealth. (Look at that last sentence. Right there is the reason why the free market has the potential to produce so much more wealth than any other economic system because it opens the door to opportunity.)

Government employees including politicians can waste fortunes in wealth produced by private sector employees. Without the incentive to produce wealth, how did Karl Marx intend for Socialism to survive? Did he even realize how important wealth creation is in a human society, in an economy?

The only way to create wealth is for the masses to have the opportunities, incentives and freedom to help themselves produce the products, markets and materials in demand by consumers, free markets.

(Offer employees a percentage of profits rather than an increase in hourly rate. If the payment system used to pay for work produced was changed from a wage paying system to a fair and aggressive incentive pay system a capitalist economy would produce much more wealth. No wage paying system could compete. An incentive pay system may also be able to maneuver around some of the Obamacare hassles.)

The liberal, socialist intellectuals are supposed to be so brilliant but the fact is that the socialist society of the Soviet Union completely destroyed itself in 50 years. I can't imagine how they can mix that into their brilliance and yet ignore the total destruction caused by socialism.

Why is it that the "brilliant" liberal intellectuals believe they are so much more intelligent than the people directly involved in the economy and yet when they take over the planning (central planning) they consistently fail so miserably? It seems socialist intellectuals stuff their brains with huge amounts of information, but they don't have the analytical ability to solve problems.

Adam Smith's remark about the "invisible hand" left a smudge of mystery about the free market. But the "invisible hand" is nothing more than "individual planning" as opposed to "central planning".

If Mr. Obama's goal of taxing wealth from the rich and subsidizing the less fortunate or less ambitious was in effect when Bill Gates created Microsoft or Steve Jobs created Apple we would not have Microsoft or Apple. They would not have had the resources or the opportunity to be so creative. None of the technological advances created in the 80's and 90's would have been created. Excessive regulations are equally destructive. Excessive taxes and excessive regulations destroy free market.

That is why Europe does not have any Bill Gates' or Steve Jobs'. The excessive taxes and regulations in Europe deprive the Bill Gates' and Steve Jobs' of the opportunity to be entrepreneurs.

The opposite effect is that the entitlements, transferred wealth, the handouts, subsidies, most Government jobs, and welfare cause perfectly capable, proud and productive individuals, including the handicapped, to become dependent on handouts and to become lazy bums, to become sheep, dependent on Government hand outs and obviously they will vote for the politicians that furnish the handouts.

There is nothing like a little hunger and hardship to stimulate ambition. Motivation! How about some reality and tough love? But first, Government must reduce taxes and regulations and bring back opportunity and free market.

A big problem in the European Union is that Northern Europe is creating the wealth and Southern Europe is spending it. Someone is going to get tired of being the sucker. Sooner or later reality is going to drag the Europeans, kicking and screaming, out of their dream world and into the real world. It's the "vision thing". But as reality starts kicking more butts, the vision thing becomes more clear. The world markets will help make the final decisions.

WHAT IS WEALTH?

Without wealth producers, NO ECONOMY CAN EXIST. (The Soviet Union is an example). The wealth producer creates the economy, the wealth producer is the economy. In order to even exist, all economies must have wealth produced by workers who create wealth by producing food, shelter, clothing, infrastructure, security and other things demanded by society. In a free market society or economy, wealth is any item that has enough demand that a price can be put on it. Wealth can be stored in other things besides currency. It also can be stored in various assets but they aren't as liquid as currency. Currency is liquid wealth.

Wealth creation is the only way to grow an economy. Reducing the value of the currency destroys wealth. Currency is wealth. Inflation is destruction of wealth.

That is why when a country is destroying its currency, the members of that society search for a country with a stable currency that they can use to store their wealth. Currency represents the stored wealth in each society. In Europe the stored wealth in each country is so diverse that it is impossible for one currency to represent them all.

Bringing back the dollar won't bring back all the wealth we have lost during the fed's massive dollar destruction but it will make the future wealth we create worth working for.

The only thing that separates the human societies from the beasts of nature is that humans have developed a system that creates wealth and stores it in what we call currency. If the currency does not represent real wealth, if the currency is diluted and its value is reduced excessively by printing and creating phony money the economy will decline. With extreme devaluation of the currency, societies will revert back to the days of the cave man.

Wealth creation is the secret to the success of all economic systems. That is why the US has been so successful for the past 100 years. But efficient wealth production has much room for improvement in all phases of wealth production. The US has potential for even greater success. All it takes is analytical, problem solving, creative capabilities and the opportunities offered and allowed by a free market.

Government does not produce wealth. Government employees, including politicians are not wealth producers. They are wealth destroyers. That is why minimum Government is the best Government. That is why reducing Government spending does not hurt the economy. The Government should never spend more wealth than the society creates.

All Governments should have a constitutional amendment that

will not allow the Government to spend more than 20% of the grand national product. It would be very beneficial for the world economy.

The wealth producer is the only person who produces wealth in any economy. Without the wealth producer there would be no wealth for the Government to transfer. There would be no economy. A worker in the Soviet Union once said, "We pretend to work and the government pretends to pay us".

The reason why Big Government doesn't work is because the only money Government has is "other people's money" and if they take too much of the workers wealth, the "other people", the wealth producers, get tired of being the sucker and stop creating the wealth. That is why Keynesians constantly try to create money out of nothing. That is why Socialism is always desperate. That is why Europe has a major crises.

HOW IMPORTANT IS CURRENCY? BASICS OF ECONOMICS.

When it boils down to the basics of economics, the name of the game is survival. It doesn't matter if you are a socialist or a conservative or somewhere in between, the truth and reality is that a society must have wealth creation and wealth production in order to survive. The main goal of all Governments should be to promote wealth production.

Economics is an interesting science. Especially when it is not excessively complicated with mathematical formulas and computer models. Humans tend to complicate and confuse the simple reality of economics. Economics is not a mathematical or mechanical science. Economics is a social science. It is about the survival of the human economic society.

Wealth creation is absolutely necessary in a healthy economy and in economics. Wealth creation is very basic and essential. When a lion kills a zebra, or a gazelle it is creating wealth. It is processing food that a whole family of lions needs to survive. When a herd of zebras travels across Africa, that herd is searching for food that the herd needs to survive, another form of wealth creation. Another example of hard work and sweating for survival.

That necessity of hard work is one of nature's laws. That necessity for hard work is the same reason why the human species created CURRENCY, for survival. With currency the human could move to a higher level. Currency set the human free to produce many forms of wealth.   With currency, every individual human no longer needed to spend all his or her time and sweat producing food, shelter and security for him or herself and family by hunting, planting and harvesting, building homes and fighting enemies.

That effort of hard work for survival is reality, that is one of Nature's laws.  The invention of money did not change that law.  Every living creature must work for his  or her own survival. That hard work is what creates self confidence, respect and responsibility in all living creatures.

That is not my theory, that is one of nature's laws.  It was a natural law long before I was born and it will be around long after I am gone.

It seems the "easy life" has allowed the human species to forget that very important law of nature, that effort of hard work for survival. And I believe the "easy life" is causing the human species to lose its ability to solve problems, its analytical ability.  Is easy living causing humans to lose their analytical ability  and causing a return to their basic animal instincts?  Analytical ability and problem solving ability are very important parts of creativity and are very important in solving economic problems, or any other problems.

The analytical ability humans used to create currency is the same creative analytical ability that sets the humans apart from other animals. Humans are the only animals that can develop analytical ability.  But when easy living causes humans to lose their analytical ability, their mental ability returns to the basic animal level.

In order to retain its value as a  MEDIUM OF EXCHANGE, the currency must represent all forms of wealth in units that are equal in value.   (It cannot be diluted with phony money printing by central banks.)  A price representing fair value is put on all items intended for exchange.  A price can be put on anything that consumers demand.  The more demand and the less supply, the higher the price.  In a free market wealth is anything consumers demand, want, need.

The human species must remember that every unit of  currency must represent something of value or it is not worth anything.  If we forget those very important basics and dilute and destroy the value of our currency with extreme, excessive money supply that does not represent real wealth we will all have to return to the survival mode of the lion and zebra.

Dumping masses of phony money into an economy will not help

anyone. It causes inflation. It will destroy an economy. Inflation of any amount destroys the value of the medium of exchange, the country's currency. Everyone suffers. It doesn't matter how great the entitlement or welfare net is.

In 1972 an ounce of gold cost $32. Today, June 2011, one ounce of gold costs over $1500. That means one dollar today is worth only two percent of what it was worth 38 years ago. In other words a dollar today is worth less than two cents compared to 38 years ago.

THAT IS INFLATION! Thank you US economists and politicians. Today inflation is rushing on faster than anyone realizes because the politicians, regulators and economists are using the wrong definition of inflation. (INFLATION Wrong definition of inflation. - Page 55)

By destroying the value of the currency with excessive money supply, it appears the expert regulators and politicians have forgotten one of the most important laws in society and economics, currency must represent real wealth. That is why at one time, the dollar was connected to gold.

Is the easy life causing these "expert" regulators and politicians to lose their analytical ability? Do Government's rules and regulations, entitlements and subsidies cause the excessive easy living? Is socialism a result of excessively easy living?

That might be negative to some people, but that is the reality, that is the truth . That is not my theory, that is nature's law. That law was around long before I was borne and it will be around long after I am gone. THAT IS THE BASICS OF ECONOMICS. THERE IS NO OTHER REALISTIC STORY.

## A WEAK CURRENCY DOES NOT BENEFIT THE EXPORTER. IT BENEFITS THE IMPORTER.

When a company exports a product and the exporting country's currency has been bashed to half its value and the importing country's currency is holding its value and remaining strong, the exporting company receives only half the value of its product. The currency may be weaker by half but the product still has the same value as when the currency was strong.

For example, if an aircraft that is worth one million dollars is exported to a country that has a strong currency that is of par value with other strong currencies and the exporting country's currency has lost

50% of its value then the importing country only has to  pay 500,000 dollars worth of it's own valuable currency for the aircraft because  the exporter's currency is only worth half its true value.  500,000 of the importing country's money is of the same value as 1,000,000, of the exporting country's money.  But the aircraft is still worth one million in true value so the importing country, on top of owning the aircraft, is also realizing 500,000 dollars of imported wealth from the exporting company and country.

How can this possibly be beneficial to the exporting company or country?  The world economists are wrong when they say a weak currency benefits exporters.  A weak currency benefits the importers.

When a country has a weak currency it exports its wealth along with its products.  The importing country benefits and the exporting country loses.  No wonder the importing country is buying from the exporting country, they are getting a bargain bonus from the exporting country.  THAT EXPORTED WEALTH IS A CONTRIBUTOR TO TRADE DEFICITS.  And it could be a MAJOR contributor to the trade deficit.

The opposite is also true, when we import products from another country and our currency is worth only half its true value, we pay twice as much as the imported products are worth.  The country that exports to a country with a weak currency is the country that benefits.  If the currency is worth only half its true value then it takes twice as much of that currency to pay for the imports.  The importing country is paying double what it would pay if the currency was at its true value.  This also contributes to trade deficits.  The fluctuation of the trade deficit lately shows that to be the case.  And it weakens the economy of the country with the weak currency.

All countries should strive to maintain a currency with a strong and steady value.  It raises the standard of living and holds down inflation.  It gives companies and consumers confidence and peace of mind and that contributes greatly to the health of the economy.  It also keeps companies from exporting wealth.  It also reduces the chance of bubbles forming.  Since the confidence of the  consumer would remain strong, recessions would be less likely to form.

The BEST FINANCIAL REGULATION any government can produce is a strong, stable currency that retains a par value with other strong currencies.

When a currency loses its value, it is the same as a tax being placed on the economy of that currency's country. If the currency is 20% below its par value with other stronger currencies, then anyone who uses the currency as a medium of exchange is paying a 20% tax on any imports they buy. The Government that regulates that currency does not realize any revenue from that tax. Only countries whose currencies remain strong and who import products from the country or export products to the country of the weak currency realize a benefit from the currency weakness. And the country with the weak currency realizes a loss of wealth.

WORLD INFLATION-CURRENCY WARS

Currency wars are a race to the bottom caused by very weak and dangerous economic thinking by central banks. World economies are spiraling downward thanks to Keynesian economics.

The world is beginning to search for a new world currency as the US federal reserve insists on destroying the dollar with junk economics, manipulating the money supply. The weak US dollar is causing currency wars around the world and has been since the US interest rate was reduced in the early 2000's.

The currency wars that countries have been introducing by bashing the values of their currencies so that they "can export more" and "not let any country get ahead of them in exports" is causing a world inflation   It is raising the prices of commodities for everyone. In fact it is raising the prices of all commodities, stocks and other assets all over the world. Currency wars are causing inflation to rise permanently. Price will not come down until the value of all currencies rise. We can thank the US Federal Reserve for this catastrophe because of their destruction of the US dollar. (See INFLATION - ANOTHER MISTAKE -Page 55)

THE CENTRAL BANKS OF THE WORLD SHOULD STOP, SHOULD DISCONTINUE USING INFLATION TARGETS TO DETERMINE THEIR INTEREST RATES. CENTRAL BANKS OF THE WORLD SHOULD REPLACE 'INFLATION' AS A TARGET WITH 'CURRENCY VALUE' AS A TARGET.

Each nation should strive to maintain a strong and stable currency that retains its par value with other strong currencies of the world. That should be the target and the goal. If the currencies of the world were maintained at a specific value with other currencies, there would be no need for a 'gold standard' as some like to say. The US dollar could retain its position as the world currency without concern from our trading partners.

The way to control the value of money is for the Central Bank to set interest rates that maintain a constant money supply and maintains the value of the currency at par with other strong currencies.

## GOVERNMENTS SHOULD STRIVE TO BE LEAN AND MEAN AS OPPOSED TO BEING BIG AND NURTURING.

Nature intended for life to be challenging. Challenges make people wise. Wise people live longer and happier. People were borne to accept challenges and solve problems. If they are not accepting challenges and solving problems, they become bored and they lose their mental capabilities.

**Only humans create an economy in any society. The human being is the only animal smart enough to create an economy and the basic tool of all economies is currency. So the subject of economics is a study of human achievement. And in any economy only the workers who create more wealth than they take home as pay, contribute to the growth of an economy.**

Most Government employees are wealth destroyers. That is why Governments should only spend money on military, security, judicial and legislative systems, items that are not attractive to private enterprise, items that are not profitable but necessary. Most Government spending does not create wealth. Realistic infrastructure is one exception. And all Government spending, including Government employee's wages is "other people's money", tax revenue created by the private investment and private wealth production.

## LEARNING THE HARD WAY

Look at the nations that were involved in the financial crises of 1997-98. They had destroyed their currencies because some world economic institutions told them they should print huge amounts of money and reduce its value so that they could export more. Their economies crashed. No one 'helped" them with loans, bailouts or stimulus spending. They had to devalue their currencies and restructure their debts. Today some of these same countries have the most successful economies in the world. It appears that the only way a society can learn is the hard way.

Germany learned the hard way when they lived through hyperinflation and default in their past. Russia learned the hard way when the Soviet Union disintegrated.

Latvia in Europe learned the hard way. Today it has one of the most successful, improving economies in Europe. China learned the hard way when their socialist system failed and they turned to capitalism. South America had several cases where their socialist systems failed and they learned the hard way.

Socialists and all socialist countries will have to wake up and face the harsh reality that all economies must have wealth and wealth production in order to even exist. No society can spend more wealth than the economy produces. Sooner or later all socialists will be forced to realize that partying on "other people's wealth", other people's hard work and sweat is not acceptable. They will have to produce their own wealth.

The poorest members of society and various poor countries will become the strongest members because the hardship will cause them to develop analytical, problem solving, creative abilities. Is that the only way societies can learn realistic economics? Is it time for the US and Europe to fasten their seat belts and prepare for the education?

OVER TIME, THE MOST SUCCESSFUL COUNTRIES WILL BECOME THE POOREST AND WEAKEST COUNTRIES BECAUSE THE EASY LIVING WILL CAUSE THEM TO LOSE THEIR ANALYTICAL, PROBLEM SOLVING, CREATIVE ABILITIES AND THE EXCESSIVE TAXES AND REGULATIONS WILL KILL WEALTH PRODUCTION AND PUSH THEM INTO DESPERATION.

A PROBLEM WITH DEMOCRACY

One problem with a democratic government is that the society becomes less analytical and capable of problem solving as time goes by because of a continuously easing and softening of lifestyles, easy living.

Due to the softening lifestyles mostly caused by constantly accumulating rules and regulations, the governing body weakens along with the society thanks to the majority rule system. The voters tend to select politicians that have attitudes similar to themselves. The politicians that are selected by the weak majority also have weakening analytical abilities. The economy begins to suffer because fewer elected politicians are capable of understanding realistic economics and economic solutions. When the weaker segment of the society's population passes beyond the 50% mark, in other words becomes the majority, the economy is doomed.

Many years may pass before economic turbulence and hardship causes the society to wise up because they can live for a long time on other people's money. Bail outs, printing phony money, cheap loans and subsidies add onto these wasted years. It appears that as democracies age, they slowly become more and more socialist. India, Europe, the US and Japan are great examples.

There are always a significant number of socialists in any Democracy. When their numbers become the majority, Socialism will become the political power. All countries that have industries that produce oil and gas are lucrative targets for socialists.

The socialist leaders are eager to take over as much of the oil and gas revenue as possible, in any way they can including taxes and nationalization. The oil and gas industry is an easy source of revenue with less political obstacles than other industries.

The socialists use this easy source of revenue to pay for so called entitlements or. more realistically, subsidies. In other words buy votes to increase political power. Venezuela, Russia, Argentina and Iran are examples.

The insurance industry is another industry the Socialists love to take over along with the oil and gas industry. They can legislate mandates and collect the forced revenue. It is even a better revenue source that collecting taxes.

The Chinese government has a lot of room for improvement but the reality is, the elderly statesmen in control have much more experience and analytical ability than younger rulers would. I believe the Chinese economy will soon be the number one economy in the world simply because of their ability to solve economic problems.

Considering the economic problems in the US, Europe and Japan, can you blame other countries for looking at Democracy skeptically? In the future will China's new leader, Xi Jinping show the world a new type of successful Governmental system?

In the past the US showed the world how productive capitalism can be. The reason why American capitalism has been copied throughout the world is because the American economies have been so successful in the past. The big question is, what kind of economic success or failure can we expect in our future? Will the world have to turn somewhere else for examples of economic success? Recently our economics and Democracy haven't been too impressive.

If dictators were intelligent enough to understand realistic economic problems and solutions, it is doubtful they would have nearly as many political and economic problems. The problem is most dictators seem to use socialist economic theories. Why is it that all dictators are socialist? Is it because they are unwilling or unable to learn realistic economics?

The problem with Socialism is that all Socialism employs unrealistic economics. If Socialism used realistic economic theories, it would not be Socialism. Even socialists can develop analytical ability if and when severe economic desperation kicks them in the butt.

"PRIVATE INVESTMENT DOESN'T WORK, IT NEVER DID!" Mr. Obama actually said that. Check it out.

In the last presidential debate in October 2012, Mr. Romney said he wanted to get private investment to creating new jobs again. In Mr. Obama's rebuttal, he said, "Private investment doesn't work. It never did." He actually said that! That was a huge statement! That goes right along with his statement, "You didn't build that". Do all Keynesians believe that? Do all socialists believe that? Do all Democrats believe that?

What does he think made the US the most productive country in the history of the world in the past 100 years? What caused all that production? It definitely was not Government investment.

What Mr. Obama is saying is, "You didn't build that, It all belongs to me and my Government. We built that." That is what all socialists and dictators are saying to the masses, "You didn't build that. It all belongs to me and the Government. We built that."

Socialists do not have the analytical ability to be creative. That is why they refuse to believe that anyone can be creative. That is why socialists say, "You did not build that" and why they say "Private investment does not work, it never did". That is why there will never be any Steve Jobs or Bill Gates in any country where Socialists are in power and will never be as long as Socialists are in power. That is why Socialism is always desperate and self destructive. Socialism does not create wealth. Socialism destroys wealth. I don't think Socialists even know what wealth is! They seem to believe currency is just a Government tool.

Since Socialists are not creative, they don't believe anyone can be creative. But if they didn't work so hard to make life as easy as possible, if they accepted more challenges, faced reality, practiced tough love and allowed a few more hardships by eliminating a slew of rules and regulations, even they could become creative.

It is amazing how educational and motivating a kick in the butt by economic hardship can be. Do we have to wait for socialist failure to find out? That can take a long time.

The only thing that improves any economy is wealth creation through private investment and workers in private enterprise producing wealth. That is why America was the number one economic power in the world for over one hundred years. That is why cutting deficits and cutting Government spending does not hurt an economy, it helps an economy.

Government spending does not create wealth. Workers such as Government workers who do not create wealth, do not help an economy grow. The wealth used to pay Government workers must be taken out of the wealth produced by the wealth producing workers in the form of taxes, (other people's money). The bigger the Government grows, the more wealth must be taken from the wealth producers to pay the Government expenses, Government waste and Government workers. That is an incentive for private enterprise workers not to produce wealth such as in Europe.

The services sector produces much less real wealth in the economy than the industrial sector. For that reason the services sector burns more wealth than it creates. It is more of a drag on the economy than a benefit. In hard times, the society cannot live on wealth produced by the services sector. You can't eat services, you can't wear services, services don't keep you warm or sheltered. In other words services are not necessary for basic survival.

Intelligent politicians that want a growing economy will always strive to create legislation that encourages wealth production.

Every unit of currency has to represent real wealth created by a wealth producer. So everyone has to produce his or her fair share of wealth. No one deserves a free ride. Money does not grow on trees. If it did no one would have to work. That is why socialism does not work.

Socialism does not work because it takes away all the wealth of the wealth producer. It takes away the very incentive for the wealth producer to produce wealth. Free enterprise, free market, private enterprise, capitalism work as long as they allow the wealth producer to retain a fair share of the wealth he or she produces. It is an incentive to produce more wealth. The more wealth a person is allowed to retain, the more wealth he or she will produce. A worker in the Soviet Union once said, " we pretend to work and the Government pretends to pay us".

If the currently accepted system of paying workers dollars per hours worked was changed to paying workers with an aggressive, fair incentive system or profit sharing, the workers would increase production significantly depending on the fairness and aggressiveness of the incentive.

One example would be private contractors being paid according to their amount of production and letting them buy their own health insurance. The increase in production is unlimited. Everyone would benefit including the workers, the owners, the Government and the economy.

History has proven that an economy where the people are more involved and the Government remains in the back ground is a much more productive economy than when the Government plays a big roll. Individual planning as opposed to central planning. The Soviet Union is an example. In fact there are several examples. China, India, Brazil and Russia have all moved away from socialism and the results are obvious. That is why, in today's successful economies the smart Governments are reluctant to get too involved.

There is a lot of difference between the "fiscal cliff" and the "sequestration". The fiscal cliff is tax increases that cause wealth producers to quit producing wealth and sequestration is reducing Government spending which reduces the wasting of the economy's wealth. Cutting taxes increases wealth production. Government spending destroys wealth.

The sequester is cutting jobs that do not produce wealth. That is not a bad thing. It is reducing Government's tendency to waste the economy's wealth.

One of the big reasons why the Democrats do not want the Government shutdown is because they are afraid the tax payers will realize that much of the Government is not needed. That is why they are making up so many unfounded reasons suggesting it will be a huge catastrophe.

A DEMOCRAT MOTO:

"Government is the only thing that we all belong to". They actually said that was their motto in the Democrat Convention of 2012. That might be true in a monarchy or a dictatorship or in socialism. But in a democracy it is the other way around. "The Government belongs to the people". That means freedom to be an individual.

IN THE US, PEOPLE DO NOT BELONG TO THE GOVERNMENT. GOVERNMENT BELONGS TO THE PEOPLE. This very major difference is what is causing the split, the partisanship between the Democrats and the Republicans. There is no middle of the road any more. The choices are socialism or free market. Do you want to be an ant, a bee, a sheep or an individual?

I have been sending letters to various congressmen from various states for several years. Recently I received a letter from a Republican congressman suggesting that my thoughts were not welcome. He said he sent my letter to my congressman in my state.

I may not be able to vote for a congressman from another state but that congressman votes for me and all other US citizens. His vote in congress does not affect only the people in his state.

The Declaration of Independence says, "A Government of the people, by the people, for the people." That means I should be able to make suggestions to any congressman. It appears they could use some thoughtful suggestions. Especially in observation of the fact that recent legislation is very unpopular and destructive as in "Obamacare" and the unacceptably weak economy.

Only Democrats, authoritarians, dictators and socialists believe in a, "People of the Government, by the Government, for the Government". They want the masses to shut up and obey, as in Venezuela, Iran, North Korea, Syria and Russia. The violence in the "Arab Spring" proves that the masses are getting tired of authoritarian rule.


SOCIALISTS BELIEVE ALL THE MONEY IN SOCIETY BELONGS TO THEM

I believe the socialists and liberals think the world owes them a living. Socialists and liberals seem to believe that the only way an economy can grow is through inflation. They create the inflation, so the money belongs to them? Do socialists and liberals believe all the money in a society belongs to them?

28

I think that all socialists and liberals actually believe that all the wealth created in the society belongs to them, and they have the right to distribute it as they see fit. Are all the wealth producers of a society doomed to be slaves for the socialists and liberals? THAT IS DEFINITELY NOT FREEDOM OR FREE MARKET!

In the Democrat's convention of 2012, they said their motto was, " Government is the only thing that we all belong to". But the Declaration of Independence says, "A Government of the people, by the people, for the people". In other words, the Government belongs to the people, a big difference. Right there is where the partisanship and big divide in Government is coming from.

The Democrats believe the people belong to the Government, Is that slavery or what? If the people belong to the Government, that means the Government owns the people. If the Government owns the people that means the people are the Government's slaves. Do all socialists believe that?

Do the socialists believe they are the masters and the rest of us are their slaves? Where is the freedom in that? Where is the equality? Where is the fairness? That is why the people on the Mayflower left Europe and wrote a Declaration of Independence and a new Constitution.

Socialism is a Government of "common good". Rules for the good of everyone and the satisfaction of none. The Government should not concentrate on "common good". The Government should concentrate on individual freedom. The choice is either individual freedom or common good. We can't have both. Which would you rather be, a bee, an ant or an individual? Everyone is an individual, no one is a group.

It seems that as people lose their analytical, problem solving ability due to easy living, they begin to believe stuffing their brains with information is all they need to make them brilliant problem solvers, "experts". That is where the "intellectuals" and "experts" come from. That is where socialism comes from.

That is why committees created by various Governments seem to be nothing more than committees of monkeys. It seems the only way socialists will learn anything is the hard way, like through hardship for example, Greece for example. End of the easy living. It seems that hardship is the only motivator that will get the masses to wise up. We could be in for a long period of weak economic conditions.

DO YOU WANT TO BE FAIR, AS THE DEMOCRATS KEEP SAYING? HOW ABOUT LIFTING THE RESTRICTIONS ON OPPORTUNIITY AND ALLOWING THE PEOPLE TO HELP THEMSELVES. If the Government will not give the people the freedom to help themselves then the Government does not have much choice but to continue paying unemployment compensation.

WHAT HAPPENED TO OPPORTUNITY? THE UNITED STATES USED TO BE THE LAND OF OPPORTUNITY.

That is why immigrants come to the US. They believe the US is the land of opportunity. And the US would still be the land of opportunity if the Government would get out of the way.

One hundred years ago a person with an eighth grade education could become rich. They didn't need an expensive education. What has changed? Back then the US was the land of "opportunity", a free market country Since then the Government has stacked on regulations and taxes, destroying the free market and opportunity. That has also destroyed small business and the middle class.

The other day I heard speeches from some Democrats on CSPAN. They all talked about the average worker. They talked about schooling and education so that the worker could become a better worker. They said they wanted to help the little guy get a better job. It seemed the Democrats felt these people were incapable of helping themselves and needed sympathy and subsidies.

I got the feeling they were talking about ants or honeybees or some other simple minded creature that could only produce a minimal amount of work. Each worker seemed to be condemned to be a slave of the system, for the system, eight and ten hour days, forty and sixty hour weeks.

Wasn't that the attitude of Karl Marx? Isn't that the attitude of all liberal socialists? Whatever happened to the American dream?

Not once did I hear anyone mention the word "OPPORTUNITY"! Whatever happened to opportunity for the individual? Sadly, I do not hear the Republicans mention opportunity either.

Immigrants do not come to the US to get a job and be a slave for the business community. They come here because they think the US is the land of opportunity. They want to become a part of the business community. They want to go into business for themselves. Every individual in the world who works at a boring job producing wealth for someone else dreams of someday having a business of his or her own. He or she does not want to work eight to ten hours a day all his or her life producing wealth so that big corporations can get rich or so politicians can take it away in taxes.

Every ambitious individual is a potential entrepreneur. When the Mayflower landed at Plymouth Rock it was full of this type of individual. The Mayflower was an example of brain drain out of Europe. The Mayflower was yesterday's immigrants and is an example of today's US immigrants.

More than any other single reason, the homeless problem is a problem of insufficient opportunity. The welfare problem is increased massively because of the lack of opportunity. Before the welfare recipient is forced off welfare he or she must have more access to opportunities or it will only add to the homeless problem and the problems of the poor.

If the political system takes away a person's ability to create wealth through excessive regulations and restrictions and also takes away his or her wealth through taxation and mandates and inflation, then the political system has the responsibility to support that person.

The politicians who create regulations that won't allow young people to take jobs as babysitters or take jobs mowing lawns and doing yard work or setting up lemonade stands may be protecting their sources of revenue but they are robbing these young people of an education in entrepreneurship. They are robbing themselves and future generations of very important revenue sources and wealth creation. These politicians are very near sighted and narrow minded and possibly a little bit selfish.

No body talks about opportunity any more. All they talk about is jobs, jobs, jobs. WHEN THE ECONOMY GETS SO BAD THAT THERE ARE NO JOBS AVAILABLE, GOVERNMENTS SHOULD REDUCE TAXES, REGULATIONS, INSURANCE MANDATES, LICENSING REQUIREMENTS AND ZONING LAWS UNTIL IT IS EASIER TO START UP A BUSINESS THAN IT IS TO GET A JOB!

Government should get out of the way. City and state rules, regulations and taxes are a major restriction to opportunity. For example, why don't cities establish areas, by changing zoning laws, where a home and a business can both be at the same address? I believe that would be a very popular area. I believe that zoning law change would reduce unemployment and the homeless problem and open up

31

opportunities for the poor. But politicians don't like that because it reduces revenue collecting opportunities.

Opportunity is the freedom and ability of ordinary people and entrepreneurs to be individuals and do their own individual planning, to help themselves start up new businesses, to be creative.

How do you find the next Steve Jobs? For the next Steve Jobs to show up, the Government must reopen the door to opportunity by reducing regulations and taxes and allow the individuals the opportunity to help themselves. When Government interference is removed, the Steve Jobs' will begin to show up.

## THE 1986 TAX CUT BILL DESTROYED OPPORTUINTY

In the 1986 tax cut bill, a part of the bill destroyed opportunity. It was the part of the bill that greatly restricted independent contractors from contracting themselves out to other businesses. That one item stopped a lot of individuals from starting up new small businesses. Throughout the US, individuals were contracting their services out to other businesses. Soon they would save up enough capital and collect enough experience to start up their own business.

The 1986 legislation stopped all this creation of small businesses and job creation. THAT WAS ONE OF THE BEST JOBS PROGRAMS THE US EVER HAD, THAT ONE ITEM KILLED OPPORTUNITY!

One of the main reasons why this legislation passed was because some of these independent contractors were not paying taxes. But once they set up business and started hiring employees they would have started paying taxes and that would have more than made up for the beginning tax loss. (Other jobs programs set up by the Government cost much more than this in tax payer money and are much less effective.)

Congress should eliminate that restriction and allow opportunity to come back to life. It would allow individuals and entrepreneurs to start up small businesses. The US economy needs that break for small businesses today more than it ever has. If people cannot get a job, they may be able to start up a small business. It would be "boot straps" legislation that would allow independent thinking, ambitious people to take care of themselves. I believe it would help reduce the homeless problem and the 'no jobs' problem.

Rather than spending trillions in tax payer dollars and phony money bailing out loser corporations, I believe, in a recession the Government should concentrate on keeping the less fortunate from enduring excessive hardship. The politicians would be doing themselves a favor.

DO YOU WANT TO BE FAIR, AS THE DEMOCRATS KEEP SAYING? HOW ABOUT LIFTING THE RESTRICTIONS ON OPPORTUNIITY AND ALLOWING THE PEOPLE TO HELP THEMSELVES.

THE AUTHORITARIANS ARE COMING

In a monarchy, the wealth producers are slaves to the authoritarians. In a dictatorship, the wealth producers are slaves to the authoritarians. In a socialist society, all wealth producers are slaves to the authoritarians.

In a democracy, the society usually starts out with a free market. But consistently increasing regulations, mandates and taxes stacked on top of each other slowly turns the wealth producers into slaves for the authoritarians. FREEDOM, WHAT FREEDOM? Forget about the civil war, the Government's authority to tax is the Government's authority to enslave.

When the authoritarians have the guns and the guns are taken away from the individuals it gives the authoritarians much more authority. In a conflict, the group without the guns suffer the largest death rates by far. All individuals should have a defense against authoritarian rule. The examples of extreme unfairness are obvious in situations such as Kosovo, Serbia, Croatia, Libya and Syria. Organizations such as The United Nations should allow the masses to have defensive methods against authoritarian rule.

REVOLUTIONS ARE CAUSED BY GREEDY LEADERS (AUTHORITARIANS) ROBBING THE WEALTH PRODUCERS SIMPLY BECAUSE THEY CAN

Nothing causes a revolution faster than when the masses see the leaders get wealthy by taking away the wealth created by the hard work and sweat of the masses or when leaders and institutions create phony money and destroy its value and through the destruction of money, destroying wealth and destroying the economy. Money is wealth and when money loses its value wealth is destroyed.

Protests are hints that the masses are getting restless. Education is a good thing because when the masses become wise they start demanding respect.  Thank you internet.

Elections are intended to expel the politicians who are not acceptable, the politicians that are selected or elected are expected to always have respect for the masses. (The reality is another matter).

Revolutions are caused by politicians (servants) who have turned themselves into authoritarians.

The conflict in Syria ( 2012) is not a civil war, it is a revolution. We are going to see more of this in countries where the authoritarians are ignoring the demands of the masses.  Thank you internet.

## THE WORLD DOES NOT OWE ANYONE A LIVING

All people born were born to produce wealth.  There never was a person born that was  so great that he or she should not have to produce enough wealth at least to support him or herself.  No one is so great that the wealth producer owes him or her a living.  Everyone must support him or herself by producing wealth in some way, either by directly producing wealth, or in some way, contributing to the production of wealth such as through  wealth supporting social services or taking care of the family.

That is nature's law.  Nobody was borne a champion.  If you want to be a winner, you have to  work harder than everybody else.

The person taking care of the family has the responsibility of teaching the family how important wealth production and hard work is. All people were born to contribute to the production of  wealth.  There never was a person born that was so great that he or she should not have to produce enough wealth to at least support him or herself.

Today, many parents do not want their children to grow up. They won't let them grow up.  That is why many baby boomers still have their fifty and sixty year old children still at home depending on daddy and mommy.  Let them grow up.  They need and would welcome some tough love and reality as young children.

The entitlement programs destroy wealth and wealth production because the recipients are receiving other people's wealth and it causes the entitlement recipients to be too lazy to produce wealth of their own because they don't have to pay it back.  That is a  slap in the face of the wealth producer.

The Government entitlement programs and  mandates make slaves out  of the people who work to create that wealth, the wealth

34

producers. Laws should be passed that makes it a crime for any Government to use tax payer's money to subsidize normal, healthy, capable individuals as a way of buying votes.

COMPASSION, KINDNESS, NURTURING? We need more of Father Nature's truth, reality and tough love.

I watched some of the Democratic convention. I was surprised to see a sea of signs. Everyone was holding the same manufactured, reproduced sign. Like a bunch of sheep. It seemed, no one had a mind of their own. So much different than the Republican convention. At the Republican convention very few were carrying identical signs. Many were carrying signs that they had obviously created themselves, such a contrast.

The Democrats are the honey and syrup crowd, way too sweet. We need more tough love and reality. I watched Michelle Obama's speech. Such compassionism, nurturism, excessive kindness. Such syrupy, dripping honey, sympathetic self pity. Such wimpiness, dishonest dream world; destructive of normal humanity. Very dangerous.

Talk like that can cause people to be afraid of reality. Talk like that will cause people to feel sorry for themselves. For a person to feel sorry for him or herself or to cause a person to feel sorry for him or herself can cause that person to lose self respect, self discipline, self determination, self control, self pride. SELF PITY, FEELING SORRY FOR ONE'S SELF CAN BE DEADLY BECAUSE IT CAN CAUSE A PERSON TO GIVE UP ON LIFE. If you want to live a long life you have to be a fighter. You cannot allow self pity. You can not feel sorry for yourself. You have to want to live.

**If everyone is kind and nurturing but everyone starts starving and freezing because no one is producing wealth, where is the compassion in that? No one is entitled to a free ride but when the Government destroys opportunity, Government is responsible for the hardship.**

It seems our society has too much compassion, kindness and nurturing. Our society needs more truth, reality and tough love. People and animals both prefer tough love to excessive kindness because tough love is more realistic. All of nature's laws are truth, reality and tough love laws. You must always be able to face reality and be honest with yourself. You can never be afraid of reality if you want to live a full

35

life.

Some times life is not fair. Some times life can be down right negative. But that is reality. Reality and truth are the same. Reality is truth, truth is reality. These aren't my theories, they were around long before I was borne and they will be around long after I am gone.

Nature's reality can just about as often be negative as much as positive. A person must be able to take the bad with the good, Man is constantly making new rules. Man made rules are all over the place intruding into everything. Natures rules are always the same, year after year, generation after generation. Nature's rules are the same all over the world.

People who tend to tell a lot of lies, lie to themselves more than they lie to others. They adjust and distort reality to help them cope with a dream world they have created. It becomes so natural, they don't even realize they are lying. They believe their own lies. They can't handle reality. That is why they get so 'bent out of shape' or defensive when they are caught in a lie. They refuse to face reality. If you consistently lie to yourself about reality, if you refuse to face reality, some day reality is going to catch up with you and that could be disastrous. The fear can be traumatic. That is what causes some people to commit suicide, the reality is too shocking.

When it becomes a matter of life or death, you either face reality or die. For example, in a socialist society when the wealth producers refuse to give the socialists their wealth or refuse to produce wealth for the socialist, the socialist either produces wealth for him or herself or starves or freezes. Motivation!

When socialists don't have access to "other people's money" they are forced to create wealth themselves. That is the beginning of an economic education, that is the end of the socialist society and the beginning of a capitalist society. That is reality. Until that happens, it appears socialism is our future.

Today, many parents are over protective of their children. The children who are pampered and protected too much by their parents and also those who are waiting around for their inheritance are the weak ones. Some parents have the attitude, "You poor child. Life is so unfair". That causes their children to feel sorry for themselves. That causes the child to be afraid of reality.

Tough love would be a better option. If you get bucked off the horse, get back on. Don't crawl under the bed and hide in fear of reality.

If you do that, fear will take over your life. But if you get back on the horse, accept the challenge and face reality you will eliminate the fear and start to develop analytical ability.

Fifty percent of the time, reality is negative, fifty percent of the time, reality is positive. That is life. You must be able to take the good with the bad. One minor problem, a person must have some analytical ability in order to even recognize reality. Sometimes it is very difficult to recognize the difference between reality and dishonesty or negativity or positive reality.

Any one can control their destiny if they really want to. It's not easy, but it's healthy. Compassion and kindness is not always helpful. Thoughtfulness is helpful, sweetness not so much. Reality can be very educational.

Excessive compassion, kindness, nurturing, or entitlements can be destructive of an individual's pride, confidence, self esteem, self respect, sense of responsibility, respect for others and ambition.

These activities rob the individual of the right to face reality, of the right to be an analytical individual. SOCIALISM IS A MAJOR CONTRIBUTOR TO LAZINESS, SELF PITY AND NON-PRODUCTIVITY. I DEFINITELY DON'T SEE THAT AS A GOOD THING. All the "intellectual" heads of socialism seem to treat people like sheep. Does socialism's subsidies and easy living turn people into sheep?

SOME PEOPLE HATE THE OPPOSITE SEX

Some people, as they grow older, develop a hatred for the opposite sex. Anyone who develops a hatred for the opposite sex should never find him or herself raising a child of that opposite sex that they hate. That child will grow up to hate society. That is where the young people who become violent and destructive to themselves and other people come from.

A SOCIALIST GOVERNMENT IS A DESPERATE GOVERNMENT.

All socialist Governments are desperate because they destroy the independent spirit, the entrepreneurial spirit, the creative spirit, the analytical ability of all the people in the society. They destroy hope and opportunity. They destroy wealth creation. They destroy free market. Through phony money creation, they destroy wealth. They turn everyone into an entitlement seeker, into sheep. They cause a brain drain problem for a society.

We need some tough love, some reality. The female animals of the wild understand the necessity of tough love and reality in raising their young. They don't get subsidies or sweet talk. Most intelligent people, male or female can understand that. Are the socialists wandering in the wilderness? Just asking. EVERY ONE HAS THE RIGHT TO BE STUPID NOW AND THEN, AS LONG AS THEY HAVE THE ABILITY TO WISE UP. People who fly by the seat of their pants have their brains in the wrong location.

One problem with a democratic government is that a continuously easing and softening of lifestyles due to continuously adding rules and regulations, subsidies and handouts causes a society to become less and less analytical and capable of solving problems. Stress used to be an educational opportunity. Today it is a health problem. The easy life style weakens mental capabilities and analytical abilities of a society.

Many men and women do not have the ability to become world leaders. They are too wimpy, kind and nurturing. You must understand the necessity of reality and tough love. Humans will never eliminate the necessity of those laws. Those are not my theories, they are reality.

The reality is, there will always be some very hard characters in the world. They do not want kindness or compassion. Kindness and compassion toward them will only make matters worse. The kindness, compassionist crowd will always be run over by the tough love, reality crowd.

Osama bin Laden once said, "when people see a strong horse and a weak horse, by nature they will like the strong horse". The US must always be the strong horse. The strong horse always does better than the weak horse.

[It takes analytical ability to anticipate the possible dangers as was present in Benghazi, Libya on 9/11/2012. No one, at the top in the US presidential administration at that time had any analytical ability. That was the problem, no problem solvers. They did not have the analytical ability to anticipate. They did not have the experience to understand. General Petraeus, head of CIA was the only one who had the abilities to prevent the disaster. But he was not making the decisions.]

## DEMOCRACIES ARE DOOMED TO SLOWLY BECOME SOCIALIST

Democracies slowly become socialist societies because Democracies, striving for the easy life and easy living cause humans to lose their analytical abilities. They lose their abilities to solve problems and their creative and entrepreneurial abilities.

Due to the majority rule of democracy, the governing body weakens along with the society. Because of the selection by the majority, the politicians that are selected will also have weakening analytical abilities. The voters tend to elect politicians who have similar outlooks. The economy will suffer because fewer elected politicians have the analytical, problem solving ability to produce realistic economics and economic solutions.

When the weaker segment of the society's population passes beyond the 50% mark, in other words becomes the majority, the economy is doomed. Many years may pass before the hardship of out of control economic turbulence causes the society to wise up. Europe and Japan are great examples. Looking at the messy economies of the US, Europe and Japan, can you blame other countries for being cautious about democracy?

The Chinese government has a lot of room for improvement but the reality is, the elderly statesmen in control have much more experience and analytical ability than younger rulers would. I believe the Chinese economy will soon be the number one economy in the world simply because of their ability to solve economic problems. If the economy is doing well and the people are being treated fairly, the society is not going to complain about not being a democracy.

## IS HEALTH CARE A BASIC RIGHT?

The subject of the right to the pursuit of happiness as stated in the Declaration of Independence, some people say that includes the right to health care.

The Declaration of Independence is not the Constitution but the Declaration of Independence can help us understand what the writers of the Constitution were trying to accomplish, can help us understand the Constitution.

In the Declaration of Independence the right to the pursuit of happiness means that the individual has the right to the pursuit of happiness so long as the individual does not victimize someone else.

When someone victimizes another individual in the pursuit of his or her happiness, the victim is having his or her right to the pursuit of happiness infringed upon.

The right to the pursuit of happiness includes the right to pursue good health and to pursue wealth so long as some innocent individual is not being victimized. But when wealth is taken from someone who does not want to contribute that wealth and transferred to someone else to pay for his or her health bills then the non consenting individual is being victimized. The Declaration of Independence was written to specifically eliminate that type of victimization. In fact, that could be considered a form of slavery. That wouldn't be constitutional would it.

No one has the right to victimize someone else for that person's benefit. That includes politicians and especially politicians. They do not have the right to select winners and losers. They do not have the right to victimize anyone, in this case victimizing them by confiscating their wealth, in order to pay for the medical expenses of someone else.

They are victimizing the people who chose to take care of their health in order to pay for the bad health of people who did not take care of their health. A very bad, negative incentive. The Government's job is to protect the individual from being victimized, not the other way around, doing the victimizing.

Mandatory insurance of any kind that forces someone to pay for some other person's expenses or profits is unconstitutional, state or federal. How about "no fault" health insurance? If I did not cause the problem, I don't have to pay. That is individual freedom. That would be fair, that would be Constitutional.

Fairness would be greatly improved if the Government produced incentives that encouraged people to develop healthy lifestyles as opposed to forcing the healthy to carry the unhealthy with compulsory insurance. That is not only unfair, that is slavery.

The main goal of the Constitution of the United States was to protect the FREEDOM of the citizens of the United Sates. Obamacare definitely does not represent freedom. Obamacare is the most anti free and unfair legislation the US Congress has ever passed.

The Government's ability to tax is the Government's ability to enslave. In the Supreme Court decision on Obamacare, the decision of one person has permanently altered the historical right to individual freedom in the United States.

I DON'T BELIEVE THE MEMBERS OF THE SUPREME

40

COURT ARE DOING THEIR JOB AS OUR FOREFATHERS HAD INTENDED.

## BOTH POLITICAL PARTIES HAVE SOME PERSONAL PROBLEMS

Both political parties have some personal problems, the crusader Republicans [is the 'pale face' worried that the Mexicans are going to take over? Is it possible the Mexicans did not 'forget the Alamo'?] and the tantrums of the "mama's boy", wimpy Democrats. Can't we all just get along?

## THE REASON WHY THE ELECTION 2012 WAS SUCH A SURPRISE TO THE REPUBLICANS.

The young employees  of the media and the social technology companies such as Yahoo!, Google and Facebook, the technology companies of Silicon Valley are college graduates that have been educated in a socialist educational environment by socialist professors , and especially in the economics department, everyone seems to be a Keynesian.

I ran into that situation when I went to college years ago. The higher education environment has become  even more socialist since then.  It seems the society's professionals have been indoctrinated into the socialist movement by a socialist education system.  In fact I think most young college graduates tend to be socialist today.   To communicate realistic economics to those people is going to be a big job. I know because my daughter is one of them.

It appears the institutions are even spending like socialists, borrowing big sums for new buildings and remodeling old ones and forcing tuition costs to rise beyond the reach of many who would like a higher education.

For the past ten years from the early 2000's to the present, the colleges and universities have hired two and three times more administrative and human service personnel than they had had previously even as the number of professors and instructors have gone down.  The extra spending is drastically increasing student tuitions. They have many excuses but I think that extra spending can be explained with two words, "socialist environment".

Another problem I think many Republicans have is that they have the attitude that they are better than everyone else simply because of their religion. They seem to think that they are the chosen people. I think that attitude turns off a lot of voters.

It seems all Republicans are hiding behind the word "Conservatism". What does that mean? What is the definition of conservatism? Is it religious, is it financial? Extreme conservative social issues turn most voters off.

It appears to me that the religious right, refusing to vote for Romney brought us the second term of Obama. Can we depend on them for more losses in the future?

Another reason why Mr. Obama won the election is because about 80% of the voters do not understand economics. The only economics they ever hear about is John Maynard Keynes. The world of economics is bigger than John Maynard Keynes.

In order for the United States economy to improve, local, state and federal politics is going to have to completely reverse course and rather than increasing and adding new taxes and regulations - eliminate old taxes and regulations. States with Republican Governments such as Wisconsin, Indiana, Texas, are the world's best economic experiment as they cut taxes and regulations. We will see if anyone learns anything.

"RULE OF LAW" MEANS NOTHING

Freedom for the individual means everything. Freedom from victimization and excessive rules and regulations.

Rules and laws are merely tools. Rules and laws can be good or bad, depending on the goals and intelligence of the creator or creators of those rules and laws. Before rules and laws are established they should be extensively debated and always have a sunset clause. When rules and laws are engraved in stone, they accumulate endlessly until they imprison a society. Freedom means freedom from excessive rules and laws. Ever heard of the Mayflower?

Man made rules are all over the place intruding into everything. Natures rules are always the same, year after year, generation after generation. Nature's laws are the same all over the world.

In a socialist Democracy, all the rules are made for the "other guy". When Socialists are in charge they make their own rules in favor of themselves in spite of the law. In older Democracies so many rules and laws are stacked on top of each other that people start to ignore them and it becomes impossible to police them all.

## ENTITLEMENTS

Entitlements, such as they are called by the people who create and promote entitlements, are not really entitlements. The promoters and creators of subsidies to the less fortunate and lazy want the subsidies to sound legitimate so they call them entitlements. They are abusing and mutilating the word entitlements   The entitlement recipients are not necessarily "entitled" to them. It is another form of welfare and vote buying.

The Government entitlement programs and  mandates make slaves out  of the people who work to create that wealth, the wealth producers. And entitlement recipients do not have to pay that money back. It is a slap in the face of free market. Laws should be passed that make it a crime for any Government to use tax payer's money to subsidize normal, healthy, capable individuals as a way of buying votes.

**No one is entitled to a free ride but when the Government destroys opportunity, Government is responsible for the hardship.**

**If everyone is kind and nurturing but everyone starts starving and freezing because no one is producing wealth, where is the compassion in that?**

## IT'S THE VISION THING

Socialist countries are desperate countries and without the analytical ability to comprehend the cause  of the downward spiral and without the ability to solve problems, the downward spiral will always happen in a socialist society sooner or later.   They will be desperate for years.

It appears that in southern climates of the northern hemisphere, life is not harsh enough (easy living) to help humans develop analytical ability.   Therefore the southerners do not develop the ability to solve problems. They also tend to become socialist countries.

Whereas in the northern climates of the northern hemisphere, the harsh (hardship) weather helps the humans to become more analytical. The northerners, such as Germany develop the ability to solve problems.

Whereas harsh desert climates cause people to develop more radical religions.   The extremely harsh and hazardous conditions of desert life contributed to the creation of the violent religions of the Arab world.   Hopefully better living  conditions will help the most extreme religions to fade away.

In the harsh desert areas of Asia and the far east, everyone has a

43

knife. Anyone can make a knife and everyone does. Similar to the US where many people insist on owning a gun. I don't think it is a bad thing, I think it is a self protection thing, a survival thing.

{When the authoritarians have the guns and the guns are taken away from the individuals it gives the authoritarians much more authority. In a conflict, the group without the guns suffer the largest death rates by far. All individuals should have a defense against authoritarian rule. The examples of extreme unfairness are obvious in situations such as Kosovo, Serbia, Croatia, Libya and Syria. Organizations such as The United Nations should allow the masses to have defensive methods against authoritarian rule}.

In the US in the past, rural areas tended to be boring because of a lack of entertainment and socializing opportunities, so religion became the main socializing event.

In the cities, there was a big variety of entertainment and socializing opportunities, so religion was less used for socializing. When technology brought computers, internet, cell phones and television to the rural areas, religion started to lose out as the main social event.

Creative opportunities and accomplishments in technology have proven to be hugely successful in the past and will continue into the distant future. Computers, internet, cell phones, television will not disappear but will evolve. The digital society is here to stay.

## ALL SOCOALIST COUNTRIES ARE DESPERATE

All socialist countries are desperate because sooner or later they always run out of other people's money. The wealth producers get tired of being the sucker and quit producing wealth. It takes problem solving analytical ability to be a leader. Socialists are not leaders, they are destroyers. I believe socialism is a self destruct system. Are socialists afraid of reality or is it that they don't have the analytical ability to recognize reality?

The leaders of socialist countries do not have the analytical ability to solve economic problems so socialist countries have to learn the hard way. Their economies have to get so bad that the hardship wises them up.

The 1998 third world financial crises helped the third world become better economists. Notice how much better the third world is doing economically today.

When it becomes a matter of life or death, you either face reality or die. For example, in a socialist society when the wealth producers refuse to give the socialists their wealth or refuse to produce wealth for the socialist, the socialist either produces wealth for him or herself or starves or freezes. Motivation! That is the end of the socialist society and the beginning of a capitalist society. That is reality. Until that happens, it appears socialism is our future.

The big divide between the two parties in the US Congress boils down to two very different goals. Those who are for socialism and those who are against socialism. Those who are living in the real world and those who are living in a dream world. Those who are facing reality and those who are afraid of reality.

SUPPLY AND DEMAND

Wealth producers fill the warehouse, (supply side). Wealth producers and other consumers, spend the wealth and empty the warehouse (demand side). If there is no wealth production, the warehouse is empty. If there is no consumption the warehouse is over flowing. Demand is just as important as supply.

Supply side economics is only half the answer. With out consumption, supply is worthless. The only way to empty the warehouse is for consumers to spend wealth. Consumers are not stupid. They know they have to have wealth in order to consume. Consumers look for opportunities to accumulate wealth so that they can become consumers.

There in lies the number one economic problem of all economies, helping the potential consumers find the opportunities. Help them become wealth producers by reducing regulations and taxes. Consumers do not want credit. They know they cannot pay the credit back until they first find the opportunity to accumulate wealth. That is why there is no demand in a recession. (Keynesians like to call this lack of demand "deflation", wrong. See INFLATION - ANOTHER MISTAKE - Page 55)

CURRENCY VALUE IS NOT DETERMINED BY THE MARKETS

Some high-powered US citizens such as politicians and regulators say that "the currency's value is determined by the markets, not the Government". Not true. The value of the currency did not change when the currency was anchored to the gold standard, no matter what happened to the markets. The markets do not change the value of the currency now.

The central bank determines the value of currency by controlling the supply. By law the Government is the only supplier of currency, controller of the money supply. And excessive supply reduces the value of the currency, inflation. An excessive shortage of supply of currency increases value, deflation. Simple reality.

The confusion comes when a stable currency is compared to an unstable currency. If the unstable currency is losing value then the stable currency can appear to be increasing in value. Not true. The unstable currency is losing value. It is the only one changing value.

The demand for currencies with a "safe haven status" can be influenced by world demand in times of financial turmoil or currency traders can change the demand for a currency but they are only changing the "world price" of the currency not the "value". It has become a world commodity.

If one unit of the currency continues to buy the same amount of goods in the "country of origin" of the currency then the "value" of the currency has not changed. The "value" of that currency does not change unless the central bank changes the supply.

## HOW ABOUT 2% DEFLATION FOR A CHANGE?

The Government's definition of inflation has not stopped inflation, it is hiding the real inflation. The real inflation is screaming on out of sight and out of control. (See INFLATION - Page 55)

Suppose that rather than trying to maintain an inflation target rate of 2%, the regulators tried to maintain a deflation rate of 2% for a while. The central bank can control inflation and deflation by controlling money supply.

## KILLING THE GOOSE THAT LAYS THE GOLDEN EGG

The wealth producing sector must have wealth and private investment, in order to produce more wealth, . When the Government takes away all of the wealth produced by the wealth producing sector it destroys wealth production. They are killing the goose that lays the golden egg.

The first four years of Mr. Obama's socialist economic theories have obviously not been good for the economy. The Republicans are trying to insert some economic truth and reality into the economy. One

46

hundred years of US economic history has proven that the Republican economic theories of free market and private investment work better. How easy we forget.

Government's responsibility is to protect the society from outside threats and to protect members of society from victimization. Governments should never go into business, competing with free market and private enterprise. The world has proven many times that Government takeover of private business does not work. It's called Socialism.

Europe has experimented with Nationalized Industries many times. South America has also experimented with Socialism. It has never worked. Free market and private enterprise is the main reason why the US has been the most productive, the most economically successful country in the world for the past 100 years. Governments are not wealth creators, they are wealth destroyers.

REDUCING VALUE OF CURRENCY DOES NOT INCREASE VALUE OF STOCKS

The feds say QE3 will increase the value of stocks. Not true! The fed's definition of inflation is not the real inflation. The fed's definition of inflation is wrong. The real inflation is screaming on, unnoticed. So the stocks and commodities and other valuable assets are not increasing in value. They are simply maintaining their value.

The fed and the analysts are wrong due to an incorrect definition of inflation. (see INFLATION Page 55) When the value of a currency drops, the prices of stocks and commodities must rise simply in order to maintain their value. Smart money sees inflation coming and buys stocks or commodities or other items that maintain their value. If they kept their money in cash, the money would lose its value. When they change their currency into assets that do not change in value just because the currency is changing its value, the investment in valuable assets then, maintains the value of their wealth as the prices of their assets rise due to inflation, the destruction of the currency. In other words, a rising stock market and rising commodities prices often means smart money is expecting rising inflation rates.

When inflation threatens, smart money gets out of cash and into strong assets just to maintain wealth. That is why, sometimes, stock earnings can be going down and stock prices are still going up. They are not cheering the fed on or worrying about profits, they are merely trying to maintain wealth and protect wealth from inflation.

And if the fed ever changes course and starts protecting the currency, (increasing interest rates, deflation), the action will reverse and smart money will get  out of strong assets and into cash because deflation will cause the prices of assets to decline as currency increases in value. The stock markets will drop.

A very large part of the increase to 13000 Dow Jones Industrial average is due to inflation.  A very large part is due to merely maintaining its value.  So when the federal reserve bashes the currency by reducing interest rates or in any other way reduces the value of the currency, such as QE1, QE2, QE3, a very large part of the increase in the stock  markets is due to the expected rise in inflation.  It is not increasing stock value, merely maintaining.  The same thing happens with commodities.  If you want to see real inflation just look at the prices of commodities.  The increase in the price and volume of  the shares of commodity ETF's from 2000 to 2012 also shows the true rate of inflation.

World economists react too much to the gyration of stock markets.  They tend to believe that when they reduce the value of the currency, they are increasing the value of stocks.  Not true!  Much of the rise in markets is due to inflation, not rise in stock value.  When  smart money sees inflation coming they get out of cash and into value stocks in order to protect the value of their wealth from inflation.

In a bull market, small caps do better than value stocks because speculators see a chance of fast profits.  In a bear market, value stocks do better than small caps because smart money sees inflation coming.

Inflation of any amount destroys the value of the medium of exchange, the country's currency.  In 1972 an ounce of gold cost $32.  Today, June 2011, one ounce of gold costs over $1500.  That means one dollar today is worth only two percent of what it was worth 38 years ago.  In other words a dollar today is worth less than two cents compared to 38 years ago.  THAT IS INFLATION!  Thank you  US economists and politicians.

What happens when so much phony money has been printed that it takes one million dollars to buy one ounce of gold?  Then the middle class will be just as wealthy as the billionaire and just as poor as the homeless because the dollar will be worthless.

The rich can maintain their wealth in inflationary times by using their extra cash to buy assets that maintain the value of their extra wealth during times when the currency is being destroyed. But the majority of US citizens do not have extra cash. They cannot do that. They have to use all their cash just to keep their heads above water. The fed's destruction of the currency is destroying the wealth of the average US citizen and reducing their standard of living. The feds are robbing the citizens of their wealth.

The Fed's policies should be just the opposite of what they have been since the early 2000's. They should be raising interest rates and raising the value of the dollar. Increasing interest rates and raising the value of the dollar would be the best "jobs program" the Government could possibly provide.

CREDIT

A society or Government should never spend more wealth (money) than has actually been created in the economy. For that reason, use of credit should be restricted. No one should be "given" credit. Everyone must "earn" credit. You should not have credit if you cannot pay it back. That is why entitlements are so unfair to the wealth producer. The wealth producer has to pay for the entitlements but the entitlement receiver does not have to pay it back. Entitlements are a slap in the face of the free market. Talk about unfairness. That is as unfair as it gets.

JOHN MAYNARD KEYNES was wrong!

What do the Democrats mean when they say the Republican's economic policies are behind the times? Do they mean to say European economics is the economics of the future? Do they call that progress? The world economy is being destroyed by socialist Keynesian economics and excessive low interest rates, phony money.

Currency wars are a race to the bottom caused by very weak and dangerous economic thinking by central banks. World economies are spiraling downward thanks to Keynesian economics.

Most of the formal economics classes of the world are teaching Keynesian economic theories and that is where the problem lies. It appears that most economists of the world study only John Maynard Keynes. That is not nearly big enough. The economics of the world is much bigger than John Maynard Keynes.

Economics is wealth creation, simple as that. Currency was intended to represent that wealth. John Maynard Keynes complicated economics because he didn't know what economics is about.

The Keynesians say Republicans have no proof of their theories on economics. I don't think anyone has less proof or facts to back up their theories than Keynesians have. In fact, I can't think of any Keynesian theories that can be proven.

When Mr. Keynes wrote General Theories in the 1930's he was not looking for realistic economic theories, He was looking for economic theories that were acceptable to the socialist leaders of Europe. As a result his theories appear to be completely unrealistic economically. Mr. Keynes was wrong, not only wrong but completely upside down with many of his theories on economics. If you want to see what happens with Keynesian economic theories, just look at Europe and Japan. Many years of no growth. Can we expect a lot more years of no growth in Europe? In the US?

## KEYNESIANS THINK MONEY GROWS ON TREES

I have been studying economics for many years. And I noticed years ago Mr. Keynes was wrong. His economic theories appear to be the old, socialist European economic theories. They don't work. They never did.

One of his biggest mistakes is that he thinks money grows on trees. Wrong! Money must always represent real wealth created by wealth producers. That is why countries with huge deficits have major economic problems. The society is spending more wealth than it produces.

Government employees, including politicians are not wealth producers. They are wealth destroyers. That is why minimum Government is the best Government. The wealth producer is the only person who produces wealth in any economy. Without the wealth producer there would be no wealth to transfer. There would be no economy. Example, the Soviet Union. A citizen of the socialist Soviet Union once said, "we pretend to work and the government pretends to pay us".

Money does not grow on trees. (Money is wealth, so wealth does not grow on trees.) If it did, no one would have to work. Keynesian theories are dream world theories. Someday soon, we are going to have to face reality.

NO ONE WOULD EVER HAVE TO WORK FOR A LIVING AGAIN!

In the hope of not having to work for a living, the human species has perpetually tried many, many times in the world's history of human economics to create money out of nothing. And to this day, as far as I know, no one has ever succeeded. What an invention that would be. No one would ever have to work for a living again.

On second thought that would not be such a good invention because no one would ever develop analytical ability again, the ability to be creative. Laziness and easy living would be the rule. All the human species would revert back to the "basic animal" mental condition that Karl Marx suggested. Human economies would disappear. Extreme Socialist desperation would spread across all human societies.

Socialists typically want to create wealth out of nothing. Either they don't want to put in the effort, or they don't know how to create wealth. But the only way they can obtain wealth is by taking it away from someone who was willing to work and sweat to create that wealth or to produce it themselves, they cannot create wealth out of nothing.

When excessive amounts of phony money are dumped on an economy, the value of the currency is diluted and the workers who create the wealth are rewarded with a currency that has lost value. In other words wealth has been destroyed. In conditions of extreme devaluation of currency, or confiscation of currency (wealth) with excessive tax rates, everyone will give up on wealth creation. This will destroy any economy.

WEALTH CREATION IS THE ONLY WAY FOR ANY ECONOMY TO GROW.

Another mistake is that he thinks an economy, in order to grow, must have a certain amount of inflation. Wrong! (And deflation scares Keynesians to death).

Any amount of inflation that reduces a currency's value below its par value with other currencies is destructive to the economy. And sometimes deflation is good for the economy.

Inflation of any amount destroys the value of the medium of exchange, the country's currency. In 1972 an ounce of gold cost $32. Today, June 2011, one ounce of gold costs over $1500. That means one dollar today is worth only two percent of what it was worth 38 years ago. In other words a dollar today is worth less than two cents compared to 38 years ago. THAT IS INFLATION! Thank you US economists and politicians.

Every time a central bank or government lowers interest rates too low or prints phony money for bail outs, stimulus or bond buying or any other creation of phony money such as 2% annual inflation, the price of gold and other commodities goes up, the stock market goes up, (much of the increase in the DOW 13,000 is due to inflation). Interest rates would also go up if the fed was not manipulating interest rates. The value of consumer items do not change just because the Government has reduced the value of the currency so the price has to go up.

The reason why the stock market jumped when QE1, 2, 3 were introduced is because 'smart money' realizes the Government activities are inflationary and causes the prices of everything to go up. They buy value stocks in order to maintain the value of their currency or wealth. Not so happy days!

'Dumb money' does not make the connection of inflation. 'Dumb money' only sees the basic moves of the interest rate cuts, bail outs, stimulus (any destruction of the currency) cause markets to jump, speculative investing. Happy days! Analysts and Keynesians tend to go along with the dumb money.

What happens when so much phony money has been printed that it takes one million dollars to buy one ounce of gold? Then the middle class will be just as wealthy as the billionaire and just as poor as the homeless because the dollar will be worthless.

What happens when the fire wall- (bailouts, stimulus and subsidies) -keeps growing until the currency becomes worthless? (The "fire wall", as in Europe, is borrowed wealth that does not exist.)

If Keynesians believe they can print all the money they need to get themselves out of trouble, why do they even bother to collect taxes? Why don't they just print all the money the Government needs and let the people keep their money?

The reason why the Government has to collect taxes is because the Government has no choice. Money must be backed up by real wealth created by wealth producers. Government cannot just print money at its convenience without destroying the currency and the economy. That is why in years past, money was backed up by gold and silver. Back then, Government economists had problem solving abilities.

The reason why Big Government doesn't work is because the only money Government has is "other people's money" and the "other people" get tired of being the sucker and stop creating wealth. That is why economic growth has stopped in Europe. That is why Keynesians constantly try to create money out of nothing. That is why Socialism is always desperate.

**For a strong economy, we must have a strong currency and low tax rates. That is obviously a big secret. That is the secret of a strong economy.**

**To strengthen the currency we must have higher interest rates. The low interest rate since 2000 proves that. US low interest rates have destroyed the US economy and the world economy. Low interest rates have destroyed the dollar and caused high unemployment. The fed bashing of the dollar is called currency manipulation. The weak dollar has caused the world currency wars.**

Currency is wealth. If the currency is destroyed, wealth is destroyed. Destroyed wealth destroys an economy. If Government spending on education, infrastructure and research improves wealth production, it improves the economy. If Government spending does not increase wealth production, the spending destroys wealth and destroys the economy.

All economies must have wealth creation in order to expand. All economies must have a strong currency to represent that wealth. The Clinton and Reagan economies had strong currencies and strong economies. The Carter and recent Bush economies and Obama economies have had weak currencies and weak economies.

If politicians are cutting regulations and Government spending but raising taxes they are creating a flat economy as in Europe. Cutting spending and raising taxes cancel each other out. If they are cutting taxes and reducing the value of the currency as they have in the US they are creating a flat economy. Cutting taxes and destroying the currency cancel each other out.

For a strong economy, Governments must promote wealth creation. They must promote strong currency and low tax rates and reduced regulations.

THE CAUSE OF THE PROBLEM (destruction of the dollar)
The single most destructive cause of the problems of the world and US economies in the past few years since 2008 is the destruction of the US dollar. It started in the early 2000's with the excessively low interest rates.

If Bush had maintained higher interest rates and maintained a strong dollar, we would not have had the real estate bubble, the financial crises or the great recession. The economy would have remained strong and Mr. Obama very probably would not have been elected in 2008.

The low interest rates and the flood of weak dollars are the cause of the problem and it appears they are going to continue to be the problem into the distant future.

THE VALUE OF A CURRENCY IS EXTREMELY MISUNDERSTOOD

President Reagan's tax cuts were a major contributor to the 1980's economic expansion. But I believe Paul Volker, in bringing back the dollar, played an equal role. In Reagan's early years they raised the federal interest rate to nearly 20% and brought back the value of the dollar. We had a great economic boom. President Bush cut taxes but destroyed the dollar with low interest rates in early 2000's. We had a Great Recession.

We had a recession in 1980. But that was because the tax cuts did not go into effect until 1982. If they had made the tax cuts effective immediately in 1980 we would not have had that recession.

In 1986 the Group of Eight world leaders decided the dollar was too strong. The value of the dollar was reduced. Five years later the US was in a recession.

The dollar was also strong through the Bill Clinton expansion. That expansion went into decline after the end of Bill Clinton's term and the beginning of the Bush term. The value of the dollar declined due to excessively low interest rates in the early 2000's. The dollar and the economy have been in trouble ever since.

In the recent Bush's 8 years they reduced the federal interest rate down to 1% and reduced the value of the dollar. We had a Great Recession. We went from Clinton's boom to Bush's recession.

We need the regulators to pull a "Paul Volker" and bring the dollar back before it's too late. Just to bring back the dollar as Paul Volker did would bring back the world economy, and especially the US economy, faster than anything else that could be done. An increase in interest rates would be the best jobs program the Government could possibly produce. Consumers love a strong currency. It raises the standard of living.

THE KEYENSIANS SAY, WHAT IF THE RECESSION CAME AND THE GOVERNMENT DID NOT SPEND TO BRING US OUT OF THE RECESSION?

The answer is, if government had maintained a strong dollar there would not have been a recession in 2008. Furthermore the wealth producers involved know much more about the problems and solutions than the Government. Government interference will only make problems worse.

The two worst economic times in the history of the US were the Great Depression and the Great Recession. Both times, the Government became more involved in the economy than at any other recession in US history.

During the times the Government DID NOT get involved the recessions remained mild.

WHAT SHOULD POLITICIANS AND REGULATORS DO TO STIMULATE A WEAK ECONOMY? NOTHING! STAY OUT OF THE WAY!

If the "too big to fail" banks that were bailed out by the taxpayers (thanks to the fed and treasury secretary) in the financial crisis of 2008 were allowed to fail and gone bankrupt instead, the banking system would have leveled out much sooner and we wouldn't have needed the Dodd Frank regulations.

INFLATION - ANOTHER MISTAKE Wrong definition of inflation.

May I humbly suggest that the estimable Keynesian masters of economics might possibly be wrong about deflation? Just suppose that they might have accidentally misplaced the definition of deflation. Suppose again that the spectacle of prices falling in a recession was not deflation at all. Could the falling of prices possibly be caused by a drop off in demand due to cautious consumer spending?

What is deflation? When the price of a gas guzzling vehicle drops because the price of gasoline has skyrocketed, is that an example of deflation? What is it- inflation- because the price of gasoline is going up or -deflation- because the prices of gas guzzlers are going down? When the price of anything falls because of lack of demand, is that deflation or merely a shortage of demand or excessive supply? It would be a tragedy if Government regulators caused further problems in the economy simply because of a misplaced definition.

Today's economists are using the wrong definition of inflation and deflation. What they call "inflation" is actually demand. When they say they are fighting inflation, they are actually fighting increased demand. When they say they are fighting deflation, they are actually fighting decreased demand. What they are doing is stepping on the gas pedal and the brake at the same time. No wonder the economy is confused.

There can never be deflation at the same time the currency is losing its value, which is inflation. That is what is interesting in economics today, the Keynesians are worried about deflation at the same time the currency is losing value. They are not looking at inflation or deflation. They are looking at supply and demand.

The definitions of inflation and deflation have nothing to do with the fluctuations of supply and demand. Supply is worthless if there is no demand and demand does not mean anything if there is no supply.

Each item, each commodity has its own price fluctuation rate due to supply and demand. The price of one item can be going up at the same time the price of another item is going down depending on supply and demand of that item. That is why price fluctuation of various items cannot be called inflation or deflation.

Inflation and deflation pertain only to the value of the currency. Excessive supply of money that does not represent real wealth decreases its value, inflation. A shortage of money increases its value, deflation.

Inflation means the currency is losing value and deflation means the value of the currency is rising. When the currency is in inflation mode the prices of all items tend to rise as long as the supply of, and demand for the items remains constant. Example, the prices of commodities. Most commodities are priced in the dollar. That is why prices of commodities and especially gold and silver have been mostly rising for the past ten years. When the value of the currency goes down, the value of commodities remain the same so the price has to rise.

And by selecting specific items to put in their basket of items used to determine their version of the inflation rate, mischievous Federal Reserves can influence their version of inflation to be higher or lower than it should be. Thanks to the feds version of the inflation rate, real inflation has been screaming on unnoticed for several years.

By using the price fluctuation of supply and demand to define inflation and deflation, they are letting the real inflation scream on unnoticed, All you have to do to see what is really going on with inflation is just to look at the price of gold and other commodities.

Inflation of any amount destroys the value of the medium of exchange, the country's currency. In 1972 an ounce of gold cost $32. Today, June 2011, one ounce of gold costs over $1500. That means one dollar today is worth only two percent of what it was worth 38 years ago. In other words a dollar today is worth less than two cents compared to 38 years ago. THAT IS INFLATION! Thank you, US economists, regulators and politicians.

When the price of wheat goes up because there is not enough wheat to satisfy demand, that is not inflation. That simply means farmers have to grow more wheat. Also when the price of wheat goes down because there is too much wheat, that is not deflation. It merely means there is more supply than demand. When the prices of gas guzzling vehicles are going down because gas prices are going up, that is not deflation or inflation.

The extreme increases in the costs of health care are not inflation. The extreme increases are due to a shortage of competition resulting from an epidemic of monopolies and probable price fixing in the health industry and extreme markups of prices due to lack of transparency and competition, especially in the insurance segment of health care. They raise prices simply because they can, they have no restrictions due to lack of competition. Shortage of competition has confusing and disruptive influence on prices, quality and supply and demand. Government mandates also cause prices to go crazy.

Inflation and deflation do not have anything to do with price changes caused by supply and demand and monopolies and Government mandates.

INFLATION AND DEFLATION ARE WORDS THAT PERTAIN ONLY TO THE VALUE OF MONEY AND DESCRIBE THE SUPPLY OF MONEY IN AN ECONOMY.

When the value of the currency of a country is at par with a basket of other strong  currencies, then the value of the currency is neither inflated or deflated. Currencies of trading partners must be at par with each other in order to accommodate easy and fair trading. When the currency retains a constant value, there is no inflation or deflation. The goal of all Governments should be to maintain the currency at a constant value and comparable to the value of other strong currencies. The gold standard was an attempt to maintain a constant value of the currency.

Forty years ago the dollar was anchored to gold and gold was at 32 dollars an ounce, That is when they disconnected the dollar from gold and let it float. (In other words, let central banks dump phony money into the economy). Today gold is over 1500 dollars an ounce. Today the dollar is worth less than 2 cents compared to forty years ago. That is what happens when politicians and regulators are allowed to create phony money. At that rate in another forty years the dollar will probably be worthless. That means very weak economy, possible devaluation of the dollar and extreme financial turmoil between now and then.

Currency is a medium of exchange all over the world. So in order to determine the value of a currency, it must be compared with values of other countries' currencies.

When central banks create phony money by increasing money supply as in bailouts and quantitative easing, they are reducing the value of the currency. That is inflation. That is destroying the currency. That is called currency manipulation. Excessive manipulation of the currency by creating phony money destroys the currency and destroys the economy.

Accusing any country of manipulating its currency is misguided. It is any country's sovereign right to control its currency. The US manipulates its currency as much as any country, and more than most.

When the US is manipulating its currency downward in order to help corporations export more, or for any other reason, it is irritating and embarrassing to hear US regulators and politicians accuse other countries of manipulating their currencies. The whole world can see what is going on. So who is the ignorant one?

Excessive money supply that does not represent real wealth causes a currency to weaken. That is inflation. When the value of a currency weakens, that does not mean the value of consumer items have to also lose their value. As a result of inflation, the prices of all products have to go up simply to maintain their value because the value of the products does not change. That is inflation.

When the prices of everything dropped in the last recession, that was a lack of demand. When there is no demand for products because people are afraid to spend, the prices tend to go down rather than up. That was not deflation. The value of the items did not change and the value of the currency did not change. The demand changed.

Japan has a similar problem. They have been fighting deflation for years. But how can they be fighting deflation at the same time their currency is inflating? It is not deflation, it is lack of demand. Big difference.

Deflation is very rare because Governments almost always create excessive money supply and almost never allow money supply to be depleted. There is always a majority of politicians that believe an excessive supply of money is better than a shortage of money. Politicians like to spend other people's money, the more the better.

And Keynesians are scared to death of what they call deflation. Many times they are fighting their idea of deflation at the same time inflation is screaming on unnoticed. But inflation is more dangerous than deflation. The threat of inflation is definitely more common than the threat of deflation.

When the currency is maintaining its value with other currencies then there is no inflation or deflation no matter what supply and demand is doing to prices. But when the currency is losing value compared to other currencies, that is inflationary. When the currency is gaining value compared to other currencies, that is deflationary.

When the value of the currency remains constant the fluctuation of prices represents supply and demand of the products. It is not inflation or deflation.

A shortage of money supply causes a currency to strengthen and is the cause of deflation. When the value of a currency increases the prices of products have to go down because the value of the products remains the same. That is deflation. In that situation stock prices go down because smart money gets out of stable assets and into the rising currency.

We could use some deflation today. The central bank would be wise to carefully reduce the supply of money rather than increase it as in QE3 and extreme low interest rates.

When the prices of things in general go down because people are afraid to spend money as in a recession, that is not deflation. That is a shortage of demand. Increasing the availability of money, as the Keynesians like to do, will not eliminate that fear. The last thing people want to do in this situation is to borrow money. People want secure jobs and healthy businesses first.

Yet increasing the availability of money is exactly what the Keynesian money managers do because they are worried about their version of deflation. That is what the Japanese money managers did in their 'lost decade'. They reduced interest rates to zero in order to increase the money supply hoping that people would start spending. It didn't work. It killed the economy and scared the consumers.

The US Federal Reserve has been trying to get people to spend money by making more money available through interest rate cuts, QE1, 2, 3, easing of credit, stimulus spending and 'strategic' bailout activity. Money supply is not the problem. Consumer confidence is the problem. If Government would quit interfering and get out of the way, confidence would come back.

People are not going to borrow or spend money until they are confident that their jobs and businesses are secure from Government interference. They are searching more for security than for money to borrow. When the economy turns around and starts to grow, the excessive money supply is going to become an instant problem. We must elect politicians that protect us from Government interference. Government interference kills free market. Regulations are the opposite of freedom. Regulations kill free market.

When the unemployment rate is normal it means the economy is producing wealth at a normal rate and wealth producers of the economy are confident that their supply of money will not run out in the near future due to loss of their job or failure of their business or interference from Government. When this happens wealth producers will start buying and hiring again.

The dependable supply of wealth or money through secure jobs and thriving businesses is their main concern. (Wealth producers are the employees, employers and independent business owners in a society, anyone producing wealth.) Government employees, including politicians do not produce wealth. They destroy wealth.

Some people like to say Government employees are the same as private industry employees because they spend money as consumers and pay taxes but the money they spend and pay taxes with is money that has been taken away from the wealth producers, the private industry employees, in taxes. They do not create the wealth themselves. And they never give any of it back to the wealth producers who's sweat created it. Is that fair?

They spend other people's money, other people's wealth. Money is stored wealth. If the money had been left in the hands of the people who created it, the wealth producers, the money would be spent much more fairly and possibly more wisely.

The service industry is a wealth producing industry as long as there is a demand for the services. But when an economy goes bad, the demand for services diminishes first because you can't eat services, you can't wear services, you can't build shelter with services.

The service industry does not produce wealth unless it is helping wealth producers produce wealth. When the service sector is hiring and the wealth producing sector is laying off workers that is not good for the economy. If the service sector is not helping the wealth producers produce wealth then the service sector is just as destructive as the Government. It is burning wealth rather than helping to create wealth.

**The retail industry should be included in the manufacturing sector rather than the services sector because retail is the final step in marketing manufactured products. Manufactured products have to be sold in order to complete the wealth creation process.**

If Governments force consumption with mandates, then it cannot be considered demand or free market and it interferes with the pricing system and the wealth involved becomes transferred wealth.

Rather than confiscating the wealth through tax increases, the Government should be helping the society produce wealth by cutting taxes and regulations and cutting spending if they want the economy to grow and jobs to be created and more revenue to be collected. Most politicians do not seem to realize how important wealth creation is.

Socialists, liberals and Keynesians do not understand how important wealth creation is. They believe inflation is the only source of growth in an economy. That is why they believe 2% inflation is necessary in an economy. Inflation is not wealth. Printing phony money to inflate the economy will not make it grow. Inflation will destroy the economy. How sad and dangerous.

Inflation of any amount destroys the value of the medium of exchange, the country's currency. In 1972 an ounce of gold cost $32. Today, June 2011, one ounce of gold costs over $1500. That means one dollar today is worth only two percent of what it was worth 38 years ago. In other words a dollar today is worth less than two cents compared to 38 years ago. THAT IS INFLATION! Thank you US economists and politicians.

SMALL BUSINESS HAS BEEN BOUGHT OUT BY BIG BUSINESS AND REGULATED TO DEATH BY BIG GOVERNMENT. THAT IS WHAT HAS DESTROYED THE MIDDLE CLASS.

That is why there are no jobs. Small business creates over 60% of all jobs. The Keynesians say Republicans have no proof of their theories on economics. I don't think anyone has less proof or facts to back up their theories than Keynesians have.

## REDUCING VALUE OF CURRENCY DOES NOT INCREASE VALUE OF STOCKS

Reducing the value of the currency does not increase the value of stocks as the federal reserve, the analysts and the Keynesians like to say. Just because the currency is losing its value does not mean stocks have to lose their value also, so when the currency loses its value the prices of stocks have to increase in order to merely 'maintain' their value. That is one reason why stock prices rise when the fed bashes the currency. Smart money moves out of cash and into valuable assets. For the smart money, it is not necessarily "happy days".

When the fed is bashing the currency as in QE1,2,3 and low interest rates, smart money sees inflation coming and changes their cash into value stocks and other assets such as gold as a way to maintain their wealth, causing value stock prices to rise. They are not looking for profits. Their main goal is to maintain the value of their wealth against inflation.

A very large part of the 14000 Dow Jones Industrial average is due to inflation. A very large part is due to merely maintaining its value. So when the federal reserve reduces interest rates or in any other way reduces the value of the currency, a very large part of the increase in the stock markets is due to the expected rise in inflation. It is not increasing stock value, merely maintaining. The same thing happens with commodities.
Actually the same thing happens with all consumer items sooner or later.

Through their monetary activities, the Feds have taken over all of the US economy and as a result also taken over the markets. (2013)

## IS INFLATION ESPECTATIONS A BIG INFLUENCE IN RISING MARKETS?

Here is an example of 'conventional wisdom' which I believe is not true. The annalists keep telling us that the investors love it when the

Fed lowers interest rates and the value of the currency drops. Because the stock market always rises when the dollar drops. I believe the analysts suggestions that investors love it when the Fed bashes the dollar is a poor analysis.

Of course there are many things that effect the direction of the stock markets. But no one suggests inflation might be an influence. I'm suggesting inflation is a big influence in the rise of markets when Fed activities reduce the value of the dollar.

I believe a big reason why the stock market rises when the dollar drops is because the smart money expects inflation when the dollar drops. Inflation causes prices to go up, even stock prices. Smart money sees threat of inflation, speculators see only opportunity for profits. The reason why I believe this is because market prices react very similarly to the prices of such inflation hedges as gold and silver.

I believe the reason why the stock market was so volatile in 2008 and early 2009 is because half of the investors believe the US economists know what they are doing and the smart money is worried more about the value of the dollar.

EXCESSIVE LIQUIDITY

Excessive liquidity is destroying the US and world economies. Extra liquidity is not the solution. Excessive liquidity is the problem. Because that 'extra' liquidity is not real wealth, that liquidity is phony money.

Low interest rates are not the solution. Low interest rates are the problem. Low interest rates cause excessive money to flow into the economy, diluting the currency. Interest rates are the main tool used by the federal reserve to control the supply of money in the economy and as a result, the value of the currency. The value of the currency cannot be batted around at the whims of the federal reserve and the Treasury or politicians. The currency must represent real wealth at all times.

The gold standard tried to maintain and hold the currency at a constant value. The reason why the gold standard won't work is because all the currencies of the world must represent all the wealth of the world and there is not enough gold and silver to represent all that wealth. We would have constant deflation problems.

What we need is an amendment to the constitution that will not allow the Government to tamper with the value of the currency. A balanced budget amendment would be helpful. The Government of a

63

society should never be allowed to spend more wealth than the society produces.

ANOTHER MISTAKE A weak currency doesn't benefit the exporter.

A weak currency may increase exports but those exports do not help the economy. If you export an airplane that is worth a million dollars and the currency has been reduced to half its value then you receive only half a million dollars for that airplane.

The importing country realizes a half million bonus. You are exporting a valuable product that does not lose its value just because the currency has lost half its value. Therefore you are exporting a valuable product plus, you are exporting half a million dollars of your economy's wealth. It is no wonder that country is ordering more products from your country. It is getting a real bargain.

How can this possibly be beneficial to the exporting company or country? The world economists are wrong when they say a weak currency benefits exporters. A weak currency benefits the importers. When a country has a weak currency it exports its wealth along with its products. The importing country benefits and the exporting country loses. THAT EXPORTED WEALTH IS A CONTRIBUTOR TO TRADE DEFICITS. And it could be a MAJOR contributor to the trade deficit.

Plus if you are importing products from that country you are paying twice as much as you would if the currency was at normal value.

That is a big reason why we have huge trade deficits with our trading partners. And a big reason why the economy is so weak. And a big reason why we must maintain a strong currency that represents real wealth.

The reason why US exporters cannot compete in foreign markets is because regulations and taxes are raising the prices of products to the point they are not competitive in world markets, not because the value of the currency is too high.

Accusing any country of manipulating its currency is misguided. It is any country's sovereign right to control its currency. The US manipulates its currency as much as any country, and more than most.

When the US is manipulating its currency downward in order to help corporations export more, or for any other reason, it is irritating and embarrassing to hear US regulators and politicians accuse other countries of manipulating their currencies. The whole world can see what is going on.  So who is the ignorant one?

## JOHN MAYNARD KEYNES
## THE BRILLIANCE OF THE LIBERAL SOCIALIST INTELLECTUAL

The liberal, socialist intellectuals are supposed to be so brilliant but the fact is that the socialist society of the Soviet Union completely destroyed itself in 50 years.  I can't imagine how they can mix that into their brilliance and yet ignore the total  destruction caused by socialism.

Why is it that the brilliant liberal, socialist intellectuals believe they are so much more intelligent than the people directly involved in the economy and yet when they take over the planning they consistently fail so miserably?  It seems socialist intellectuals stuff their brains with huge amounts of information, but they don't have the analytical ability to solve problems.

Milton Freedman once said. "we are all Keynesians now".  Most economists of the world today believe in John Maynard Keynes' theories of economics.  But his theory of Governments printing phony money to avoid financial crises is destroying the  world economy.  The Japanese have practiced Keynesian theories for twenty years and their economy has gone nowhere for those twenty years.  Europe is drowning in phony money.

If the Keynesians believe they can print all the money they need to get the country out of trouble, why do they bother to tax the people.  Why don't they just print all the money they need and let the tax payers keep their money?

The reason why the Government taxes the people is because the Government does not have a choice.  All money must be backed up by real wealth produced by the wealth producers.

Most Government workers, including politicians, do NOT produce wealth, therefore they are not wealth  producers. They are carried by the taxes on the wealth producers.   And politicians are responsible for the taxes and regulations that restrict wealth production.  Politicians are responsible for the bailouts, stimulus's, irresponsible spending and loans, entitlements and subsidies that wastes the wealth of the society.  Politicians and Government employees destroy wealth.

Lets see there is a million, billion, trillion.   What comes after trillion?  At the rate Government is printing phony money we are going to be there very shortly.

## THE WORST TAX IN THE WORLD, THE CONSUMPTION TAX

As far as the economy is concerned, the consumption tax is the most deadly tax in the world because consumption is the economy. The economy is consumption. Without consumption there is no economy. Societies cannot exist without an economy or without consumption. The consumption tax destroys the incentive to consume, it is an incentive not to consume. No society should ever establish a consumption tax. It interferes with the demand side of economics.

The consumer is the economy. Governments, in other words, politicians must give the consumer more respect.

Once a consumption tax is in place it is almost impossible to get rid of because the politicians love it so much. That is why it should never be introduced in the first place.

A consumption tax is deadly. It grows until it destroys an economy. A consumption tax is like a cancer. It grows into every phase of the economy. It gets into the raw material level. It gets into the manufacturing level, the wholesale level, the retail level of the economy. If you want an economy to be prosperous you do not want to retard consumption with a consumption tax.

Consumption tax, sales tax, value added tax, national sales tax, they are all bad. They are  destructive to any economy. But the consumption tax is the worst.

In England the consumption tax rate is almost 25%. An extreme incentive not to consume. Most European countries have  consumption taxes.  Most of their economies have problems. Japan passed a consumption tax in the late 1980's. The people of Japan were strongly against a consumption tax. Japan passed it anyway. Japan's economy has gone nowhere for twenty years. Japan and Europe are examples of what a consumption tax can do to an economy.

A consumption tax is a socialist tax. The consumption tax is an ideal tax for a socialist society, that is as long as they do not care if they have a weak economy. It helps them collect wealth from all phases of the economic process.  One of the most important things Japan and England can do to help their economies is to get rid of the consumption tax

A 25% consumption tax, that's more than the rate of profit that most businesses make on their efforts. And the Governments grab that wealth without any respect for the sweat effort involved in creating that wealth. How can the Governments possibly deserve more of the wealth created than the businesses and workers who created it? Talk about destructive confiscation! They do it simply because they can.

EUROPE

AUSTERITY AND TAX INCREASES - EUROPEAN TROUBLES

It seems almost impossible to take Socialism out of a European. It seems Europeans believe Socialism is the only way. Margaret Thatcher tried and failed. If she couldn't do it I don't think anyone can.

Latvia should thank their citizens for NOT throwing a tantrum because they lost their subsidies as some of the Southern Europeans did. Latvia did the right thing by cutting expenses and regulations but they should not have raised taxes. If they had not raised taxes their economy would have improved even faster and their young brain power would not be leaving.

One of the biggest economic problems in all of Europe is excessively high taxes. Europe is going to have to cut, rather than raise taxes if they want real wealth creation and growth in the economy. In Europe the word is "growth". (What kind of growth are they talking about, economic growth or social growth? They have been too successful with their social growth.) But they will never get economic growth by raising taxes and increasing regulations and mandates on wealth production or by creating and spending phony money.

In Southern Europe the rates of return on various bonds are gyrating up and down, but that is just a panic barometer. The real problems are not going away until Southern Europe starts producing its own real wealth.

Governments are spending too much of other people's money, especially southern governments. Government should never spend more wealth than their society produces. But they are wrong to demand more revenue by increasing taxes if they want growth. Excessive taxation and regulation in Europe is all ready interfering with wealth production and growth and it has been a problem for a long time.

The Europeans say their problem is a competitiveness problem. What are they competing for? They are competing for wealth. The indebted countries are competing for the wealth of the thrifty countries and the thrifty countries are getting tired of being the sucker.

67

Someone in Europe once said, "the Euro never was primarily an economic creation". They said the European politics were more important than the currency. WRONG. Politics are always flexible and changing, currencies represent wealth. Currencies are always and primarily economic creations! The currency IS the wealth in a society. The currency is the economy. That is the reality.

The simple reality in Greece is that a society cannot spend more wealth than it creates. That is Europe's number one problem, they don't understand the importance of wealth production. That sounds like a political problem to me.

A big problem in the European Union is that Northern Europe is creating the wealth and Southern Europe is spending it. Someone is going to get tired of being the sucker. Sooner or later reality is going to drag the Europeans, kicking and screaming, out of their dream world and into the real world. It's the "vision thing". But as reality starts kicking more butts, the vision thing becomes more clear.

As the restrictions on individual planning increase and taxation, transfer of wealth and restrictions on production of wealth increases, the brain power and wealth will flow out of the society. The remaining people in the society will become lazier and less wealth will be produced. The economy of the society will decline and hardship will increase. If a strong, socialist, dictator type Government does not lock the society into Socialism, the society will demand that the Government change back to free market.

The European Union has part of it right -austerity. But they are wrong about tax increases. Tax increases are not austerity. Tax increases reduce growth and wealth production and increase Government spending. Tax cuts are austerity because they help reduce Government spending. Tax cuts increase growth and wealth production and help to reduce Government spending.

Austerity means cutting Government spending, in other words, reducing the size of Government. Governments do not create wealth. Governments destroy wealth. Reducing spending, regulations and cutting taxes are examples of austerity and the only way to reduce the size of Government. The Europeans have been raising taxes as much as they have been cutting spending. That is not austerity. The Europeans are stepping on the gas pedal and the brake at the same time. No wonder they have no growth, no wonder they have a crisis.

Socialist societies have a problem creating wealth. They don't understand how important wealth creation is in an economy. That is why most socialist societies do not last very long. Socialist societies are going to have to face reality. For Southern Europe this is a reality check. We will see if they learn anything. Germany has already had a reality check.

Some talking heads in the Governments of Europe and the US are saying some European economies should raise the wages of workers so that they can consume more. I am skeptical of their true goal. Do they want the worker's wages raised so that the Governments can raise their taxes? How about keeping the worker's wages the same and lowering their taxes? It would be the same benefit for the consumer or worker. Also lower wages would keep prices down and exports more competitive. Governments must not spend more wealth than the economy produces. All countries should have a balanced budget amendment in their constitution.

JAPAN-
ECONOMIC PROBLEMS.

Japan says they are fighting deflation. For over twenty years they have been fighting deflation. The problem is it is not deflation, it is a shortage of demand, a shortage of consumption! Japan's Keynesian economics have kept Japan in recession or near recession for over twenty years. The economy is weak because demand is weak. The economic weakness is caused by Keynesian economics. You cannot have deflation and a weakening currency (inflation) at the same time. Japan should try something NEW, like increase interest rates, like increase the value of the Yen. Consumers love a strong currency.

Japan has been having a reality check for over twenty years. They don't seem to be learning anything. Japan installed a consumption tax and cut interest rates 5 times in 5 years, between 1985 and 1989, down to zero. Today the rate is still zero and the consumption tax has been increased. Japan has had two lost decades.

In order for an economy to grow a society must produce more wealth than it uses. The only way for any economy to grow is for Government to give the private sector incentives to produce wealth by reducing regulations and taxes. Then if the Government gets out of the way and does not interfere, confidence and demand will come back.

As the Government increases taxes to pay for Government expenses, the wealth producer realizes less take home pay and profits.

As the tax load increases the incentive to produce wealth is destroyed. Obviously the economy will suffer. This is the problem in Europe and Japan. Over taxed wealth producers are refusing to produce wealth, destroying economies. It will happen in any society where taxes are too high and regulations are too restrictive.

The wealth producing sector must have wealth and private investment, in order to produce more wealth. When the Government takes away all of the wealth produced by the wealth producing sector it destroys wealth production. The faster the Government takes away wealth and the more wealth the Government takes away from the private sector, the faster the Socialist society will self destruct. Especially when crony capitalism and corruption is involved. They are killing the goose that lays the golden egg.

The speed at which Government confiscates wealth determines the time it takes for Socialism to self destruct. As long as some wealth producers continue to produce some wealth the Socialist Democracies can limp along for many years enduring a weak economy. Japan is an example.

Government employees, including politicians are not wealth producers. In fact they are wealth destroyers. Construction of infrastructure is one exception. The only way that construction of infrastructure will benefit an economy is if the new infrastructure improves the efficiency of the society and helps it produce more wealth. Bridges to nowhere and digging holes and filling them back in are totally wealth destruction activities.

EXCESSIVELY LOW INTEREST RATES CAUSE BUBBLES. BUBBLES CREATE FINANCIAL CRISES.

An excessively low interest rate allows excessive money supply into the economy. Other excesses may also cause bubbles but excessive money supply is the most common cause. A bubble is too much demand chasing a shortage of supply, too much money supply chasing a shortage of product.

The Federal Reserve is the one Government agency that has all the necessary tools to prevent all exuberant bubbles from forming. It should lean toward maintaining a strong currency as opposed to creating a weak currency to benefit exporters, or a low interest rate in order to placate investors or financial institutions. Unwise Federal Reserves create bubbles.

WHAT HAPPENED?

Was the world financial crises of 2008 caused by US Government regulators?

The economic misery that the whole world experienced between 2007 and 2009 was caused by the US Federal Reserve keeping the short term money-market interest rate too low for too long between 2000 and 2009. If they had maintained a strong dollar by keeping interest rates higher the excessive money supply would not have materialized.

This opened up the window for loan companies to grab up masses of cheap money. The major world crises, the housing bubble and the extreme economic problems would not have materialized if the US Federal Reserve had concentrated on maintaining a strong dollar as opposed to lowering interest rates.

We would still have a respectable economy today if the Central Bank had not lowered interest rates in 2000 and kept them low. There would not have been a world financial crises and Mr. Obama very probably would not have been elected in 2008.

Lenders will inevitably think of ways to take advantage of the excessive money supply or liquidity. When the interest rate was kept too low for too long in the early 2000's the lenders scooped up this excessive supply of low interest money and developed schemes to loan it out any way they could.

THEY PROMOTED EXOTICALLY DESIGNED ADJUSTABLE RATE MORTGATES TO EVERYONE. IF THERE HAD NOT BEEN IRRESPONSIBLE LENDERS THERE WOULD NOT HAVE BEEN IRRESPONSIBLE BORROWERS.

They bundled these shaky mortgages in packages and sold them to investors as a way to distance themselves from these low quality contracts.

If the Federal Reserve had not kept the interest rate so low for so long, the loan industry would not have grabbed up such huge amounts of this cheap money (enough to create a housing bubble), there would not have been such an excessive supply of low interest money for the lenders. Without the money, the lenders would not have been able to create the real estate bubble.

The Federal Reserve made a big mistake by not keeping higher interest rates and by not maintaining a strong dollar.

If the Loan industry had not grabbed up the cheap money and

pushed it onto the uninformed in any manner possible, such as adjustable rate mortgages, etc., there would not have been a real estate bubble. This is what caused the real estate runaway. This is what brought the economy down on our heads!

THIS IS WHAT CAUSED THE FINANCIAL CRISES! WITHOUT THAT EXCESSIVE SUPPLY OF MONEY THE WORLD WOULD NOT HAVE HAD THIS FINANCIAL CRISES!

THE FEDERAL RESERVE INCREASES MONEY SUPPLY BY LOANING THROUGH THE DISCOUNT WINDOW.

The Federal Reserve creates money. The Federal Reserve controls the money in circulation, the money supply. One of the ways the Fed regulates money supply is by setting the interest rate at the discount window. Through this window the Federal Reserve loans out money to banks and thrifts, the loan industry. The Federal Reserve does not loan this money to individuals. The financial institutions, the loan industry, loans out the money to individuals. Those loans to those financial institutions is what increases the money supply.

High interest rates means less money supply because interest is the price of money and when the price goes up the demand goes down. Low interest rates means a larger supply of money in circulation.

The excessively long period of the Federal Reserve's low interest rates in the early 2000's invited the Loan industry to borrow as much of this cheap money as they possibly could.

The Loan industry makes money by borrowing at a cheap rate and loaning it out at a higher rate. They also make money by adding fees and commissions to each loan.

They also make money by using leverage. Using leverage is very risky and one of the causes of the financial crises. When their leveraged investments are working as planned they make fast money. But when the investment plan goes wrong they lose money fast because of the leverage.

The Government should never bail them out. The Government should only be concerned with the harm to the innocent. THE ONLY WAY CAPITALISM CAN WORK IS FOR THE RISK TAKERS TO PAY THE PROPER CONSEQUENCES FOR THEIR UNSUCCESSFUL RISKS. That is fair and reasonable because when the risk taking is successful, the risk taker collects the high rewards. The Government should put in place reserve requirements and regulations that keep risk takers and leverage users from getting too exuberant and that protect the innocent from harm.


RISK

No one should be allowed to take excessive risk with "other people's money". Excessive leverage and risk don't mix. Risk takers should only risk their own money.

But risk must not be eliminated. Risk taking is a very important part of any healthy economy. Risk is the oil that lubes the capitalist system.

It might be wise to restrict leverage but otherwise leave risk alone! Don't regulate it, don't subsidize it, especially do not insure risk or bail out risk takers. Insuring risk reduces the educational effect of risk. Let it do its job! Alongside of mistakes, risk is one of the greatest teachers in the world. But the Government should force the risk takers to suffer the consequences of their risks. The Government should protect the innocent from being victimized by the risk takers.

Risk is one of nature's tough love rules. Risk forces a society to be analytical and creative. Without risk a society becomes mentally lazy. The people lose the ability to solve problems and to be creative. That is why insuring risk and bailing out risk takers does more harm than good.

Governments and politicians cannot regulate risk, they don't even know what risk is. All they do is complicate and destroy the action. Only markets and consequences can regulate risk.

WHAT HAPPENED TO CONFIDENCE?

Government interference destroys confidence. When the economy gets bad and the Government decides to bail out a corporation or intervene in some other manner, all private planning and trading slows down and adjusts, expecting more Government unpredictable interruptions. The people stop planning and dreaming because they don't know what the Government interruptions will do to their plans and dreams.

In a good economy the people have plans and are constantly adding new plans. Even in an economy that is not so good, wealth producers (employees, employers and independent business owners) working in the economy continually produce plans and ideas that they will incorporate into the economy. The plans that work are passed on. The ideas that do not work are discarded.

That is the normal action of economies as long as the Government allows the wealth producer to retain a fair share of the wealth he or she produces. Incentive is extremely important in capitalism. The wealth producer must be allowed to retain a fair amount of the wealth he or she creates as an incentive to produce more wealth. That is the basics of capitalism! That is what makes an economy grow.

The wealth producer produces onward through the necessary and unnecessary restrictions, regulations, taxes, zoning laws, bailouts, fluctuation of money supply, insurance mandates, etc as long as they are allowed to retain a fair share of the wealth they produce. Unnecessary interference sometimes drags an economy to a halt. Sometimes Government interference reduces or even stops wealth production. Examples, southern Europe and Japan and lately, the US.

If the Government was not so quick to intervene, the private market would do much more to bail itself out. The market is constantly planning and adjusting. But when the Government intervenes all the planning and adjusting is interrupted.

If the Government allowed the economy to correct itself the economy would rebound much quicker and the economy would experience less damage. And the wealth producer would have a learning experience. When the Government intrudes it causes confusion that prolongs the slump. And it appears the intrusion itself is confused. When the Government regulators periodically throw out trial balloons of interference into the economy it causes confusion and slows the recovery process.

When the Government intervenes and the intervention does not work, which happens too often, the people become cautious, especially when the intervention includes regulations, mandates, tax increases, subsidies, bail outs, QE 1, 2, 3, interest rate cuts, and the value of the currency declines.

I don't believe the economists or politicians realize how much a weak currency affects the confidence of the consumer. When the currency loses value the people lose confidence. Consumers love a strong currency. A weakening currency can cause a recession all by itself. A weakening currency reduces the standard of living and the people feel this. Everything costs more. It is similar to a tax increase.

It is destruction of wealth. Central banks should have more respect for the consumer or possibly be more restricted by Congress.

When a recession starts, sometimes the Government steps in. If the intervention works everything is fine. Shaky Government intervention that doesn't work causes people to lose confidence. More often the intervention does more harm than good.

If the economy gets worse, the Government intervenes some more. If that doesn't work, the people become more cautious and a new idea is tried by the Government and so on. It becomes a chain reaction, a snow ball effect which results in confidence being completely destroyed. People stop planning and dreaming and start saving. Jobs are lost, businesses close and spending stops. Recession or worse are the results.

WAS THE CRISES THE RESULT OF REGULATORY PANIC AND \ OR CONFUSION? WAS THE REGULATION AND BAIL OUTS NECESSARY \ UNNECESSARY?

('August 1, 2009', is the reason the economic crises is bottoming out right now simply because the volume of Government interference has significantly receded? Have they run out of ideas and money, are they suffering from the shock of the recession?) Is the reason why the Government regulators cannot predict the coming recessions and crises and bubbles because they are the cause of these recessions and crises and bubbles?

The Government's 'top notch' regulators dump these shaky fixes onto a weakening economy much too quickly, without any idea what would happen if they gave the economy time to adjust itself. If the wealth producers involved in the economic activity were allowed to make the adjustments and corrections, they would learn from their mistakes and move on and the economy would move back to normal. Plus, the people involved in the action probably know a lot more about the problems and the solutions than the Government regulators do.

THE FED'S MANDATE OF KEEPING INTEREST RATES LOW IN ORDER TO INCREASE EMPLOYMENT IS HAVING THE OPPOSITE EFFECT. The Fed's expect low interest rates to somehow keep people employed. If low interest rates keep people employed as the Federal Reserve says, why has extremely low interest rates since 2000 allowed unemployment to double and stay high for the past ten years? It appears low interest rates have the opposite effect. It appears low interest rates cause unemployment.

The Federal Reserve claims that low interest rates will help people find jobs and lower the unemployment rate. But it is so obvious, the whole world can see that in the past few years (from 2006 to2012) the result has been the exact opposite of the Fed's claim. It is impossible to miss the reality. In fact it is more realistic to say lower interest rates caused the unemployment problem.

The regulators are going to keep interest rates low because the unemployment rate is too high. But the unemployment rate is so high because the interest rates are so low. When the US regulators try to use the interest rate to influence the unemployment rate, that is similar to the dreams of chasing rainbows.

Keynesians say easy money causes growth in the economy. Just looking back at the financial policies the last few years in Europe and the US proves that they are wrong. In fact the complete opposite is true. The countries cannot spend more wealth than the society creates. The currency must remain strong.

THE FED'S MANDATE OF KEEPING INTEREST RATES LOW IN ORDER TO INCREASE EMPLOYMENT IS HAVING THE OPPOSITE EFFECT. RAISING THE VALUE OF THE CURRENCY WOULD BE THE BEST "JOBS PROGRAM" THE GOVERNMENT COULD POSSIBLY PRODUCE. They could start by increasing interest rates.

When the Government bashes, destroys the currency and reduces its value with bail outs, quantitative easing, subsidies, stimulus, and extremely low interest rates the unemployment remains high and the economy suffers. These Government activities are not the solution, they are causing the problem. Unemployment is high because interest rates are too low. Several years of this activity has proven it to be obvious. Why is it so difficult for some people to see?

The feds say that the past quantitative easing has saved two million jobs and accelerated growth but they have no proof. The reason why they say this is because they realize there is no way to prove them wrong. The reality is very probably the opposite. If there actually was economic and employment gain as they say, it was probably in spite of the fed's actions.

MISTAKES AND RISK TAKING ARE NOT ONLY NORMAL BUT NECESSARY IN A HEALTHY ECONOMY.

Mistakes are as important as successes. People learn much more from their mistakes than their successes. Mistakes are the most productive educational tools ever invented. If the Government does not allow people to learn the full lesson from their mistakes, everybody suffers.

BUT THE PEOPLE HAVE TO WAIT UNTIL THE GOVERNMENT RUNS OUT OF IDEAS AND MONEY AND THE CONFUSION SUBSIDES BEFORE THEY CAN GET BACK TO THE JOB OF PRODUCING WEALTH. SINCE THE GOVERNMENT CAN CREATE PHONY MONEY AS IF THEY WERE PICKING FRUIT OFF A TREE AND CREATE REGULATIONS AS IF THEY WERE PLAYING A VIDEO GAME, THAT CAN TAKE A LONG TIME.

THE QUESTION IS; will the spending and the bailouts the Government has been distributing recently produce more wealth than the amount spent? (2009) If it does it will be beneficial for the economy. Governments very seldom spend money that creates more wealth. Governments do not create wealth.

But if the Government's recent spending produces less wealth in the economy than the amount spent, then the spending was a waste and the economy will still improve in spite of the spending but the wasted wealth will be a drag on the economy.

But the economy will only continue to improve if the Government remains in the background. If the Government continues to interfere in the economy, for example by hastily adding damaging new regulations such as health plans and business regulations to the economy or continues to beat up on the dollar or raises taxes, we could still see a long stretch of weak economic conditions for a long time or even a DEPRESSION.

The confidence of the people is the most important part of any economy. The consumer is the economy. If there was no consumer there would be no economy. If there was no wealth producer there would be no economy. The Government must get out of the way and let confidence return.

## GOVERNMENT INTERVENTION CAUSES ECONOMIC SLUMPS TO BECOME RECESSIONS AND DEPRESSIONS.

The regulators involved in Government intervention say that some unacceptable scenario such as complete collapse and chaos will happen if the Government does not get involved and do huge bailouts. But they are either unwilling or, more likely, unable to describe that scenario. No one knows what would happen if the Government did NOT intervene.

In fact I don't think they know what will happen when the Government does intervene. Is there more collapse and chaos when they do intervene? Are they interfering in order to defend their jobs?

I believe that if we can get past the fear of complete collapse and chaos predicted by these prominent economists and regulators, a recession where the Government does little or nothing may not be nearly as bad as we are led to believe. In fact, I believe Government intervention may very probably make matters worse. Government intervention destroys the confidence of the people. Especially when it doesn't work. Government interference caused the Great Depression and the Great Recession.

The Federal Reserve chairman keeps saying the Fed had to do what they did (low interest rates and bailouts in 2008) in order to prevent total collapse of the financial system. But they never give us an example of what that total collapse would look like. The reason they do not give us an example is because there is no example. They really don't know if there would be collapse or improvement if they did not interfere. (It seems their main goal is preserving their jobs).

In the mild recessions of the past the Government did not intervene. I believe the recessions were mild because the Government did not interfere.

The two worst economic times in the history of the US were the Great Depression and the Great Recession. Both times, the Government became more involved in the economy than at any other recession in US history, huge Government interventions.

During the times the Government DID NOT get involved in the recessions, all the recessions remained mild.

WHAT SHOULD POLITICIANS AND REGULATORS DO TO STIMULATE A WEAK ECONOMY? NOTHING! STAY OUT OF THE WAY!

When the economy gets bad and the Government decides to bail out a corporation, all private planning and trading slows down and adjusts, expecting more Government interruptions. The people stop planning and dreaming because they don't know what the Government interruptions will do to their plans and dreams.

If the Government was not so quick to intervene, the private market would do much more to bail itself out. The market is constantly planning and adjusting and fluctuating . But when the Government intervenes all the planning and adjusting is interrupted.

If the Government allowed the economy to correct itself the economy would rebound much quicker without wasting tax payer money. When the Government intrudes it causes confusion that prolongs the slump. And it appears the intrusion itself is confused. When the Government regulators periodically throw out trial balloons of interference into the economy it causes confusion and slows the recovery process and wastes tax payer money.

When the economy starts to turn downward , the Government should not be too quick to intervene because the market very probably all ready has plans to do something about it. It is very probable that the people involved in the problem areas know much more about the situation than the Government does.

And if some of the business managers don't know what is going on, let them fail and let the strong ones take over. That is how the economy is supposed to work. That is an incentive to get it right. That is a learning experience, very educational. That is how economies grow and prosper.

It appears the Government regulators believe they are the only ones who know how to respond to a crises. Does their response make the crises worse, or possibly even create the crises? Does the Government have to run out of ideas and money before the economy will turn around?

It seems that all the prominent US economists are reading from the same book. They all have the same old ideas. If the solution to some unusual economic problem is not in the book, they are lost. Then they usually dream up some interference that makes the problem worse.

First the economists tell us we don't save enough. Then they tell us we have to spend and borrow more. And back and forth. It seems they don't know which way they want it. Maybe they don't understand that spending and saving are two opposite directions. And we depend on them to solve the financial crises or the economic crises? How about the possibility that their solutions create the financial crises and economic crises.

In the recent past when the Federal Reserve reversed its trend of increasing interest rates and began its latest rate reduction (I believe it was September 2008) the stock market initially jumped but then reversed and took a major drop.

What would have happened if rather than reducing the interest rate, the Fed had 'raised' the interest rate a quarter percent instead. It would have been a surprise. I believe the stock market would have dropped initially but then reversed and started climbing. I doubt the market would have fallen nearly as low as it did in 2008 and early 2009.

The reason the market would have shown enthusiasm for a rate increase is because the consumers were beginning to be concerned about the value of their currency. The consumer is the economy. The Federal Reserve should have more respect for the consumer.

When the currency loses its value the consumer is the one who gets hurt the most. When the currency loses its value the standard of living drops because the consumer has to pay more for everything. This is a major reason for the consumer's lack of confidence. This is a major reason for the slump in demand. This can cause a recession.

## THE MAIN GOAL OF GOVERNMENT REGULATIONS SHOULD BE - FIRST, DO NO HARM

The Government should be very careful about interfering in the gyrations of the economy

The best thing the Government can do is maintain a stable, strong currency and let the economy fluctuate.

The Federal Reserve is the one Government agency that has all the necessary tools to prevent all exuberant bubbles from forming. It should lean toward a strong currency as opposed to excessive money supply and a weak currency.

The Government should be very careful about legislating new regulations on the market and the economy. Government regulations are the cause of many of the market's and the economy's problems.

## BALANCED BUDGET AMENDMENT

All Governments should have a balanced budget amendment because all economies can only spend the amount of wealth created by the wealth producers in that economy. To spend more than the real wealth that is created in the society causes deficits. The society is living beyond its means. All medium of exchange must represent only real wealth. A Government that creates phony money that does not represent real wealth is causing inflation and is destroying the economy. A Government that borrows excessively causes deficits to grow out of control.

The debt ceiling is a weak attempt to control Government spending. Controlling Government spending is an important, healthy goal. But in order to actually control Government spending, some type of constitutional amendment must be enacted. A society should never be allowed to spend more wealth than the society actually creates. (Greece is a good example). Various types of national crises may be a temporary exception.

All value or wealth, is produced by the wealth producer. Property has no value without a wealth producer's labor. Land increases in value with the wealth producer's labor creating a building or producing a crop or extracting the gold or oil. Ownership does not produce value. The labor of the wealth producer produces value and wealth. However, ownership through shrewd speculation can take advantage of changes in property value.

TODAY THE GOVERNMENT SPENDS TRILLIONS OF DOLLARS LIKE IT WAS ONLY PAPER? AND THE GOVERNMENT TELLS US THERE IS NO INFLATION?

What kind of dream world are they in? Excessive low interest rates, excessive money supply and an excessively weak currency create INFLATION! Inflation is another way of saying weak currency. Is their inflation target 'slightly' manipulated? Is there another bubble in our near future? [See INFLATION - Page 55)

Inflation of any amount destroys the value of the medium of exchange, the country's currency. In 1972 an ounce of gold cost $32. Today, June 2011, one ounce of gold costs over $1500. That means one dollar today is worth only two percent of what it was worth 38 years ago. In other words a dollar today is worth less than two cents compared to 38 years ago. That is INFLATION! Thank you US economists and politicians.

## INCREASE IN THE VALUE OF THE CURRENCY ENDS A RECESSION

In the early 1970s the dollar was released from a gold standard. There was already too much money supply in the economy and the dollar was under pressure to devalue or inflate. Price controls were even put in place trying to control inflation.

Then in the late 1970s the Government regulators wanted the money supply increased further and interest rates were lowered causing more inflation pressure. The dollar was still seeking its true value due to its disconnect from the gold standard and that is what caused the inflation rate to be so erratic in the late 70's. The value of the dollar bounced around trying to find its true value, gold shot up to 800 dollars and silver shot up to 50 dollars. I believe the disconnect from the gold standard was the main reason the inflation rate was so high and erratic at that time.

**One of the best recoveries from a recession was when President Carter replaced the Federal Reserve Chairman with Paul Volker a few months before the end of Carter's term in 1979. Mr. Volker raised interest rates to nearly 20% and brought back the value of the dollar. The economy did very well after that and after President Reagan's tax cuts took effect.**

**But then in 1986 the group of eight world powers decided the dollar was too strong and decided to reduce the value of the dollar. They did reduce the value of the dollar and this brilliant move caused a recession in the early 1990's. It caused the removal of the Republican from the White House and replaced him with a Democrat. President Clinton brought back the value of the dollar and the economy did very well.**

## SUPPLY AND DEMAND

Wealth producers fill the warehouse, (supply side). Wealth producers become consumers, spend the wealth and empty the warehouse (demand side). If there is no wealth production, the warehouse is empty. If there is no consumption the warehouse is over flowing. Demand is just as important as supply.

Supply side economics is only half the answer. The only way to empty the warehouse is for consumers to spend wealth. Consumers are not stupid. They know they have to have wealth in order to consume. Consumers look for opportunities to accumulate wealth so that they can become consumers.

There in lies the number one economic problem of all economies, help the potential consumers find the opportunities, help them become wealth producers. Consumers do not want credit. They know they cannot pay the credit back until they first find the opportunity to accumulate wealth. That is why there is no demand in a recession.

SUPPLY SIDERS and producers like to see a small amount of inflation and more monopolies in the economy because it means higher prices and more profit.

Consumers, or 'DEMAND SIDERS' like to see a little deflation and more competition because it means lower prices and more opportunities and jobs.

We have heard so much about the supply side of the economy from economists. What about the demand side of the economy? It is just as important as the supply side.

Politicians should pay more attention to the demand side because there are a lot more voters on the demand side than the supply side. Republicans tend to represent the supply side and Democrats tend to represent the demand side.

Consumers are the demand side. Consumers love a strong currency. Consumer confidence is necessary for strong economic growth.

The Government regulators are excessively concerned about deflation. The consumer would love to see a little deflation. Consumers would like to see prices come down. Suppose that rather than trying to maintain an inflation target rate of 2%, the regulators tried to maintain a deflation rate of 2% for a while.

In a deflationary time the value of the currency rises. But the value of assets would remain constant so prices would have to go down in order to merely maintain asset value. So there would be a tendency for bear stock markets and the prices of commodities would tend to go down as smart money got out of assets and into the rising currency

IS PHONY MONEY BEING CREATED BY FINANCIAL INSTITUTIONS?

(May 2011) Most of the wealth producing industries are not producing much wealth right now, due to the weak economy. The economy has almost totally stopped producing wealth and interest rates are near zero. Virtually no one is borrowing money. Loaning money to the private sector is supposed to be the main source of income for financial institutions. Yet the financial institutions are making obscene profits.

How can this be? The only answer I can see is that they are creating tons of phony money with their computerized financial programs and their insurance and phony reinsurance schemes, borrowing money from the Government and then buying Government instruments. And that is helping to reduce the value of the dollar even further. They are not creating wealth. It might be profits, but it is not wealth.

The so called too big to fail financial institutions are not creating wealth, they are creating phony money. Their profits are an illusion.

There is a law that says only the Government is to create money. That is one of the big reasons why a society needs a Government; to separate the real wealth from the phony money.

MONOPOLIES

TOO BIG TO SUCEED! WHAT EVER HAPPENED TO THE ANTITRUST AGENCY?

The excessive accumulation of the so called "too big to fail" corporations that over populate the US economy tells me that the Government has totally abandoned antitrust responsibility. Due to Government negligence, or maybe even assistance, the US economy is overloaded with monopolies. For example, regional monopolies as in the oil industry, industrial monopolies as in the medical and drug industries and national monopolies as in finance and insurance.

These monopolies are the major cause of the high prices in gasoline and medical care and also contributed to the financial crises. These monopolies are pricing US products out of the world markets. These monopolies are allowing corporate CEO' s to way overcompensate themselves.

These monopolies are allowing corporations to hire mediocre CEOs and board members because they don't have any competition to force them to be efficient. These monopolies are more destructive to job creation and do more harm to the economy than outsourcing of jobs to foreign countries. Mergers and acquisitions destroy more jobs than they create because their goal is to reduce overhead and create monopolies. THESE MONOPOLIES ARE DESTROYING THE ECONOMY!

**In 1980 CEO pay was 42 times more than the average worker. Today, 2013, CEO pay is 354 times more than the average**

worker.  After Mr. Regan became president in1980 he encouraged mergers, acquisitions, buyouts and allowed monopolies to form and didn't pay any attention to antitrust regulations.  The merger and acquisition craze has been screaming on ever since forming monopolies all over the US.  Monopolies don't have any competitive restriction that forces CEOs to hold down their ridiculously extreme salary arrangements.

COMPETITION IS THE ONLY WAY TO KEEP CAPATALISM HONEST.

Competition protects the free market from the excessive greed of capitalism.  Monopolies destroy that competition.  Capitalism loves monopolies but monopolies are not free market.  Companies in monopolies are more like nationalized companies.  Most mergers and acquisitions destroy more jobs than they create.

These monopolies are reducing the number of small businesses and, in turn, destroying the middle class.  SMALL BUSINESS HAS BEEN BOUGHT OUT BY BIG BUSINESS AND REGULATED TO DEATH BY BIG GOVERNMENT.  THAT IS WHAT HAS DESTROYED THE MIDDLE CLASS.  Small businesses produce more than 60% of the jobs in the US.  Small business owners make up a large part of the middle class.

In the  medical industry alone the prices of prescription drugs are marked up so extremely that it is an insult to human intelligence.  Because they do not have enough competition or transparency, thanks to the Government regulators such as the FDA and the monopolies in the medical industry.

Competition forces all competitors to maintain competitive prices and highest quality.  Competition would keep management from paying themselves obscene salaries and benefits.  They do it because they can, because they have no competition.  Some of these oversize, inefficient conglomerates would begin to disappear if the Government would encourage and allow lean and mean competition to exist and if the Government would enforce antitrust regulations.

AND IF THE GOVERNMENT WOULD ALLOW LOSERS TO FAIL!

If the feds and the treasury had allowed the financial institutions to fail and go bankrupt in 2008 we would not have seen the financial crises and the economy would be back to normal today.  That is the way a capitalist market is supposed to work. That is the only way a free market can work, a competitive market free from monopolies and excessive Government interference.

Due to lack of competition the management of monopolized companies don't have to be competent or be efficient. That is why top management in these loser corporations is so mediocre and so over paid. From CEO to pizza delivery, how significant is that? It has happened! They can raise prices and they don't have to deliver any quality products, (except quality pizza), because they  have eliminated competition. They use cheap quality materials to produce their products. They give themselves all sorts of wild and excessive perks, bonuses, fees and salaries simply because they can, simply because they do not have competition to keep them efficient.

City, county and state managers, employers and employees see the obscene wages, salaries and perks that these freewheeling corporate managers pay themselves and determine that these local managers and employees are way underpaid. They demand higher compensation according to the corporate example. That is one of the main reasons why so many state  budgets have such  major problems. If Government regulators allow it, corporations will buy up all companies that might be a competitive threat, or they run them out of business creating a monopoly. That is why we have an antitrust department.

Only stiff competition will force capitalists to be efficient and responsible and management to be competent. Competition forces them to keep prices down and quality up. THE CONSUMER IS THE MAJOR BENEFACTOR OF COMPETITION. COMPETITION AND BANKRUPTCY ARE THE BEST REGULATIONS ANY ECONOMY COULD EVER HAVE.

If corporations were not allowed to buy up or eliminate competition, the competition would force the companies to hire competent, capable and efficient management, force management to accept a reduced, realistic salary, increase quality of products and reduce prices. Exports would be more competitive and there would be less outsourcing of jobs.

HIGH GAS PRICES, REGIONAL MONOPOLIES

Also, corporate competitors in the gas station industry in two different regions swap their business operations in the competitors regions for the competitors businesses in their own region creating regional monopolies. I saw this happen in the oil industry in the early 1990's. I thought at the time, 'what a way to create a monopoly and raise prices'. Most of the mom and pop gas stations also disappeared at around that time.

COMPETITION IS THE BEST REGULATION CAPITALISM WILL EVER HAVE. COMPETITION IS THE ONLY WAY TO KEEP CAPITALISM HONEST.

Eliminating the competition through favors from politicians, buyouts, lobbying and practicing crony capitalism is common practice today. Examples include bail outs, quantitative easing, stimulus, choosing winners and losers, practicing favoritism with regulations, bashing the currency and especially, Government mandates, Government loans, Government cronyism with special interests and Government allowing monopolies. THESE ACTIVITIES ARE VERY DESTRUCTIVE OF FREE MARKETS AND ECONOMIES. CAPITALISM CAN EXIST IN ALL OF THESE CONDITIONS, FREE MARKETS CANNOT.

CAPITALISM LOVES MONOPOLIES BUT MONOPOLIES ARE NOT FREE MARKET Markets cannot be rational , efficient and self regulating unless they are free markets, free of monopolies and open to fair competition.

It is a typical goal for capitalism to eliminate, suffocate, eradicate competition. However, capitalism cannot realize its full potential without competition in a free market. In order to have the most productive, healthy economy, the Government must insist that capitalists do not eliminate competition. Free, competitive markets increase job opportunities and business opportunities. Monopolies are similar to Government nationalization. Monopolies destroy economies and free markets.

Monopolies give competitive foreign companies huge opportunities to supply products to the US, a big reason for outsourcing. If the Government allows monopolies, then the Government must allow foreign competition. If you don't want outsourcing and sending jobs overseas, then you must eliminate monopolies. If you don't want corrupt capitalism and overpaid management then you must eliminate monopolies.

The US health industry problems are an example of capitalism running out of control. It appears to me that the health industry is trying

87

to keep the masses uninformed and sick (among other things) so they can realize maximum profits.

Of course the Government must use smart regulations to prevent the greedy from becoming too exuberant. Maintaining a strong, stable currency, using antitrust regulations and bankruptcies, allowing competition to eliminate monopolies and regulating leverage and increasing capital reserve requirements are some examples of smart regulations.

## WHAT WOULD A GOOD GOVERNMENT LOOK LIKE?

A good Government would not allow monopolies to destroy a free market. A good Government would not destroy free markets with excessive interference. A good Government would remove regulations that did not work as expected.

A good Government would be one that protects a society from foreign invasion or terrorism. A good Government would maintain a competitive free market where demand and supply was relatively balanced and the currency remains at a constant par value with other strong currencies. With a currency that maintains a constant par value with other strong currencies, inflation, deflation, recessions and bubbles should not become a problem.

A good Government would allow wealth producers to take risks, but would not allow the risk takers to harm the innocent. A good Government would allow an economy to solve its own problems with minimal amount if interference. That kind of Government would produce a healthy free market and a strong economy.

## NATIONALIZED COMPANIES

Lack of competition is one major reason why nationalized companies are not as successful as private companies that exist in free markets. Without competition, nationalized companies do not produce competitive products and their operations are inefficient. A nationalized company is a company owned and run by the Government.

Also in nationalized companies, the incentive factor is missing. The incentive to make a profit. The incentive factor is what makes capitalism work. The wealth producer will not produce wealth either if he or she does not have an incentive. In capitalism, INCENTIVE has much more potential value than society and the Government regulators realize.

Also in nationalized companies, central planning takes over and eliminates individual planning. Central planning slows progress and creativity and the nationalized company cannot keep up with individual planning of capitalism.

Governments do not produce wealth. Their workers have no incentive to produce wealth. Governments also do not have the mental capabilities necessary to produce wealth. If governments need wealth they take it from the wealth producer, "other people's money".

In order to produce a healthy economy, a wealth producer must produce more wealth than he or she consumes or spends, otherwise the wealth supply will shrink until there is no wealth and no economy left. THAT IS WHY SOCIALISM DOES NOT WORK.

That is why the Soviet Union went broke. A worker in the Soviet Union once said, "we pretend to work and the government pretends to pay us".

History has proven that an economy where the people are more involved and the Government remains in the back ground is much more productive than when the Government plays a big roll. The Soviet Union is an example. In fact there are examples all over. China, Russia and India have all moved away from socialism and the results are obvious. In today's successful economies the smart Governments are reluctant to get too involved.

However, in some cases nationalized companies are more desirable than companies that have created a monopoly. Because companies involved in monopolies also do not produce competitive products. Companies that are involved in monopolies actually perform similar to a nationalized company, incompetent, inefficient and have mediocre, incompetent management because they do not have competition. And for these same reasons they produce low quality, high priced products. These products are not competitive in world markets.

The Government should not bail out the poorest performing companies. The Government should do the opposite, protect the best performing companies from fallout caused by the miss management of the losers. Let the losers fall. Let the system self correct. Usually the losers brought the problems onto themselves. This type of regulation won't do nearly as much damage to the confidence of the consumer as the bail outs do. This type of regulation would be much easier on the budget deficits.

# BANKRUPTCY

I hear people saying we do not have enough regulations. But we do have regulations, very effective regulations. They are called bankruptcies. But the regulators won't allow them to work. If we want capitalism to work, we must allow bankruptcies to do their job.

The regulators basically ignored this regulation. The regulators are doing more harm than good. It seems bankruptcies are not compassionate enough. The regulators are destroying our economy with kindness. That is a socialist hang up. We must face reality.

BANKRUPTCY IS ONE OF THE BEST REGULATIONS CAPITALISM WILL EVER HAVE! It injects a very important dose of reality into the system. If the US Government wants the US economy to be strong and competitive in the new world economy, the US Government must face reality.

Bailing out the losers with billions of tax payer dollars is not fair to the strong companies. It does more harm than good. Bailing out the weak companies gives them a cushion and an advantage that they do not deserve. It gives them room to lower prices and steal business from their competitors and helps destroy confidence. It contributes to the monopoly disaster. It destroys free market. Bailouts are subsidies to the losers, a reward or incentive for being a failure. IF YOU DON'T LET THE LOSERS FAIL, YOU ARE DESTROYING THE FREE MARKET.

It is also quite obvious that the regulators doling out the bailout money are too cozy with the top brass of the conglomerates. Many of the Government regulators are selected from the management of conglomerates.

In some instances it appears Government even restricts competition and encourages monopolies to form.

# GOVERNMENT AND CORPORATE CRONYISM

Antitrust action should NOT be decided on a politicians desire to punish a company for making campaign contributions to the wrong political party or other similar political reasons. Politicians should not be allowed to select winners and losers. Insufficient competition that allows a company to raise prices without competitive restrictions, and especially if the company actually raises prices excessively should be the main reason for determining antitrust action.

## STATE AND LOCAL GOVERNMENTS CAN BE DESTRUCTIVE TO SMALL BUSINESSES

It seems small businesses have enemies in every branch of Government. But State and local governments are even more restrictive. Their regulations, restrictions, taxes, fees, insurance requirements, licensing requirements and zoning restrictions can be very destructive to small business start ups and entrepreneurs and kill opportunities for small business start ups and make it very difficult for startups to survive and small companies to succeed.

This is a major reason why we have minimal competition for bigger companies and a reason why so few jobs are being created. This is a major drag on any economy, good or bad.

Small businesses as a group create many more jobs than big corporations do. Small businesses produce more than 70% of the jobs in the society. At least they used to.

Mergers and acquisitions do not create jobs, they reduce jobs. Creating monopolies does not create jobs, it reduces jobs. And as the large corporations buy up the small businesses and companies, that means less and less job creation and more job reduction. Government should not protect companies from competition and should not encourage mergers and acquisitions. Competition is a 'must' for a free market.

I believe a severe shortage of small businesses in the US is the main reason why new job creation has been so weak the past ten years, 2000 to2010. Small businesses are the middle class. Fewer small businesses, fewer middle class.

Many entrepreneurs and creative wealth producers in our society do not realize their potential because they do not have the necessary financing or facilities, and there are excessive regulations and taxes. They are too busy trying to survive. In some cases Government should help, possibly by reducing taxes and regulations. .

I believe the Government should go so far as to help create competition against monopolies by reducing regulations and giving tax breaks and low interest loans and subsidies to potential competitors as opposed to adding regulations and other restrictions in order to protect their existing revenue resources or in their incorrect opinion that they can protect the little guy with more regulations. Government should go back to its old job of restricting and breaking up monopolies and encourage competition.

The wealthy people of our society are not the most creative people of our society. In fact the opposite is generally true. The poor and unfortunate of our society tend to be more creative and analytical simply because they must endure hardship and solve the problems caused by the misfortune and hardship.

The biggest problem the poor people have is that they are so busy making a living they do not have time to be creative. The reason why people like Bill Gates and Mitt Romney are so successful is because they had monetary support that gave them the freedom to be creative.

SCHOOL OF HARD KNOCKS

Small businesses and start ups don't usually hire college graduates. They usually hire high school graduates, high school drop outs and college drop outs, people who will accept low wages because small businesses are educating and training these people on the job. The school of hard knocks is also an expensive education system. There is a huge supply of this type of individual in the US. They need jobs too!

But the insane idea of increasing the minimum wage is forcing these people to become "entitlement recipients" because excessive high wages are destroying start up businesses and small businesses or keeping them from starting up to begin with or keeping them from hiring these people. This is another cause of the downward spiral of the US economy.

There are two minimum wage rates in the US, the Governments minimum wage rates and the realistic, zero minimum wage rate, no job. The higher the Government minimum wage rate, the more people join the zero minimum wage rate bracket.

ENTREPRENEURSHIP IS OPPORTUNITY, OPPORTUNITY IS ENTREPRENEURSHIP

If Mr. Obama's goal of taxing wealth from the  rich and subsidizing the less ambitious or less fortunate was in effect when Bill Gates created Microsoft or Seven Jobs created Apple we would not have Microsoft or Apple. They would not have had the resources or the opportunity to be so creative. None of the technological advances created in the 80's and 90's would have been created. Excessive regulations are equally destructive.

That is why Europe does not have any Bill Gates' or Steve Jobs'.

92

The excessive taxes and regulations in Europe deprive the Bill Gates' and Steve Jobs' of the opportunity to be entrepreneurs.

The opposite effect is that the entitlements, transferred wealth, the handouts and subsidies and welfare cause perfectly capable and productive people to become dependent on handouts and become lazy bums. There is nothing like a little hunger and hardship to stimulate ambition.

WHAT HAPPENED TO OPPORTUNITY? THE UNITED STATES USED TO BE THE LAND OF OPPORTUNITY.

The other day I heard speeches from some Democrats on CSPAN. They all talked about the average worker. They talked about schooling and education so that the worker could become a better worker. They said they wanted to help the little guy get a better job. It seemed the Democrats felt these people were incapable of helping themselves and needed sympathy and subsidies.

I got the feeling they were talking about ants or honeybees or some other simple minded creature that could only produce a minimal amount of work. Each worker seemed to be condemned to be a slave of the system, for the system, eight and ten hour days, forty and sixty hour weeks.

Wasn't that the attitude of Karl Marx? Isn't that the attitude of all liberal socialists? Whatever happened to the American dream?

Not once did I hear anyone mention the word "OPPORTUNITY"! Whatever happened to opportunity for the individual? Sadly, I do not hear the Republicans mention opportunity either.

Immigrants do not come to the US to get a job and be a slave for the business community. They come here because they think the US is the land of opportunity. They want to become a part of the business community. They want to go into business for themselves.

Every individual in the world who works at a boring job producing wealth for someone else dreams of someday having a business of his or her own. He or she does not want to work eight to ten hours a day all his or her life producing wealth so that big corporations can get rich or so politicians can take it away in taxes.

Every individual is a potential entrepreneur. When the Mayflower landed at Plymouth Rock it was full of this type of individual, all immigrants. Every pale face in the US is the result of immigration. The only difference between then and now is that laws were passed that made immigration illegal.

More than any other single reason, the homeless problem is a problem of insufficient opportunity. The welfare problem is increased massively because of the lack of opportunity. Before the welfare recipient is forced off welfare he or she must have more access to opportunities or it will only add to the homeless problem.

If the political system takes away a person's ability to create wealth by imposing excessive regulations and restrictions and also takes away his or her wealth through taxation and mandates then the political system has the responsibility to support that person and the economy will obviously decline.

The politicians who create regulations that won't allow young people to take jobs as babysitters or take jobs mowing lawns and doing yard work or setting up lemonade stands may be protecting their sources of revenue but they are robbing these young people of an education in entrepreneurship. They are robbing themselves and future generations of very important revenue sources. These politicians are very near sighted and narrow minded and possibly a little bit selfish.

Nobody talks about opportunity any more. All they talk about is jobs, jobs, jobs. WHEN THE ECONOMY GETS SO BAD THAT THERE ARE NO JOBS AVAILABLE, GOVERNMENTS SHOULD REDUCE TAXES, REGULATIONS, INSURANCE MANDATES, LICENSING REQUIREMENTS, FEES AND ZONING LAWS UNTIL IT IS EASIER TO START UP A BUSINESS THAN IT IS TO GET A JOB! Give the people the opportunity to help themselves.

City and state rules, regulations and taxes are a major restriction to opportunity. For example, why don't cities establish areas where a home and a business can both be at the same address? I believe that would be a very popular area.

Opportunity is the freedom and ability of ordinary people and entrepreneurs to start up new businesses, to be creative.

In the 1986 tax cut bill, a part of the bill destroyed opportunity. It was the part of the bill that greatly restricted independent contractors from contracting themselves out to other businesses. That one item stopped a lot of individuals from starting up new small businesses. Throughout the US, individuals were contracting their services out to other businesses. Soon they would save up enough capital and collect enough experience to start up their own business. The 1986 legislation stopped all this creation of small businesses and job creation. THAT WAS ONE OF THE BEST JOBS PROGRAMS THE US EVER HAD, THAT ONE ITEM KILLED OPPORTUNITY!

One of the main reasons why this legislation passed was because some of these independent contractors were not paying taxes. But once they set up business and started hiring employees they would have started paying taxes and that would have more than made up for the beginning tax loss. (Other jobs programs set up by the Government cost much more than this in tax payer money and are much less effective.)

Congress should eliminate that restriction and allow opportunity to come back to life. It would allow individuals and entrepreneurs to start up small businesses. The US economy needs that break for small businesses today more than it ever has. If people cannot get a job, they may be able to start up a small business. It would be "boot straps" legislation that would allow ambitious people to take care of themselves. I believe it would help reduce the homeless problem and the 'no jobs' problem.

Rather than spending trillions in tax payer dollars and phony money bailing out loser corporations, I believe, in a recession the Government should concentrate on keeping the less fortunate from enduring excessive hardship. The politicians would be doing themselves a favor.

DO YOU WANT TO BE FAIR, AS THE DEMOCRATS KEEP SAYING? HOW ABOUT LIFTING THE RESTRICTIONS ON OPPORTUNIITY AND ALLOWING THE PEOPLE TO HELP THEMSELVES.

Another Government practice that hit small businesses and the middle class was that in the 1980's the Government ignored antitrust laws more than ever before. Big business was allowed to buy up small businesses without antitrust restrictions. That reduced competition. That was the beginning of a rash of new monopolies. The monopolies were a big cause of the destruction of the middle class. Big corporations, buy outs and new monopolies do not hire nearly as many new workers as small businesses do. In fact they usually lay off more workers than they hire because of the consolidation.

Small businesses and start ups don't usually hire college graduates. They usually hire high school graduates, high school drop outs and college drop outs, people who will accept low wages because small businesses are educating and training these people on the job. There is a huge supply of this type of beginning worker in the US. They need jobs too!

But the insane idea of increasing the minimum wage is forcing these people to become "entitlement recipients" because excessive high wages are destroying start up businesses and small businesses or keeping them from starting up to begin with. The school of hard knocks is also an expensive education system. This is another cause of the downward spiral of the US economy.

## FREEDOM TO TAKE ADVANTAGE OF OPPORTUNITIES

Many handicapped people are very capable and able to be even more productive than people who are not handicapped and those people are very proud and confident.

Politicians should not be so willing and anxious to take away the wealth of the wealth producers in order to subsidize and give handouts to the less fortunate (and possibly lazy) and the handicapped because subsidies and handouts destroy their natural instincts of independence, pride, self preservation, confidence, responsibility and productivity and turns them into lazy bums, dependent on the handouts, entitlements and subsidies. It changes them from individuals to sheep.

Government employees that do not help to produce wealth are also carried by the wealth producer. They develop the feeling that they deserve the handouts, they deserve to be carried by the wealth producers. The demonstrations in Wisconsin and Greece were examples of this. During hard times this is not a sustainable situation in any society.

And when the Government takes away the wealth produced by the wealth producer in taxes and gives handouts and subsidies to the non wealth producers, it is destructive to the productivity of the other side, the people who produced that wealth. It destroys the incentive to produce wealth. The economy is the loser. Everyone is the loser.

Governments should not take over, control or try to run businesses. Governments do not produce wealth. Governments should concentrate on expanding opportunities and free markets by reducing taxes and regulations and the masses will produce the wealth. That is how to create a thriving economy.

A huge problem with many Governments, including democracies and dictatorships is that the leaders do not understand economics. Workers and business owners learn realistic economics on the job by producing the wealth in an economy. The school of hard knocks is the best economics education a person can get. If workers are given incentives to produce wealth and allowed to retain a fair share of that wealth, there would be no revolutions or riots and the economy would prosper.

The masses are looking for opportunity. Opportunity to own property, to set up businesses, to be entrepreneurs, to create their individual life styles, to provide necessities for their families, to accumulate wealth, freedom to dream and plan, the freedom to help themselves.

Education is not the answer. Freedom to take advantage of the opportunities is the answer. Less subsidies, transfers of wealth, rules, regulations, taxes, bail outs, stimulus's, entitlements, more free markets, more opportunities. Governments should depend more on competition to regulate markets. Governments should not allow monopolies. Monopolies eliminate competition. Competition is the best regulator an economy can have. And Government should allow businesses to fail. Tough love!

Give the masses the opportunities and freedom to help themselves and the economies will prosper. And the condition of being poor will be greatly reduced.

Leaders of Socialist countries and liberals and socialists in general do not understand economics, they do not know how to create wealth, they do not understand how important wealth is in an economy. Economies must have wealth creation in order to even exist. Government workers do not create wealth. A society made up of only Government workers is a dead society.

The only way to create wealth is for the masses to have the opportunities, incentives and freedom to help themselves produce the products, markets and materials in demand by consumers, free markets.

Educated young people all over the world are restless. Where are all the jobs and opportunities? Obviously education is not the answer. Obviously Governments do not create jobs. In fact Governments destroy jobs because they destroy opportunity. The US used to be the land of opportunity. But we don't hear anything about opportunity any more. All we hear is jobs, jobs, jobs. Everyone is supposed to work for someone else like a bunch of honey bees.

Governments must get rid of regulations, rules, restrictions, excessive taxes, licenses, zoning laws, subsidies, stimulus's, bailouts, etc

97

that do not work. It seems the Government refuses to eliminate any of their experiments that do not work. They keep adding restrictions on top of restrictions until the economy is constipated. Government must get rid of this economic straight jacket.

Governments must bring back opportunities and allow people to help themselves.

The Government takes wealth away from the wealth producer in taxes. The only money the Government has is "other people's money" (unless the Government creates phony money by lowering interest rates too low or prints phony money with the money presses as in QE 1,2,3). Then the Government loans that tax money out to the loan industry through the discount window. The loan industry loans the money the Government originally lifted from the wealth producer back to the wealth producer. The money does not belong to the wealth producer any more. Now the wealth producer has to pay back with interest the wealth he created in the first place.

The money the Government lets the wealth producer keep in tax cuts goes directly into the pockets of the wealth producer. The wealth producer does not have to pay interest on the money and the wealth producer doesn't have to pay the money back.

SPECULATION

In 2008, I watched the charts of commodities and a chart of the dollar. When the value of the dollar went down the price of commodities went up. When the value of the dollar went up the price of commodities went down. The reaction was immediate. It didn't take weeks, days or even hours for the reaction to occur. Within minutes nearly all commodities responded.

Commodities are demanded by all the countries of the world so their prices are controlled by world demand. But commodities are priced in dollars so when the value of the dollar goes down prices of commodities have to go up in order to maintain a constant and stable world price. That was an example of real inflation believe it or not.

There was a lot of speculation because most investors know that when the value of the dollar goes down the prices of commodities and stocks go up. That is about as predictable and reliable a trade as can be found and traders know that; result, speculation. The problem is not speculation. The problem is Fed bashing of the currency.

EVERYONE WHO TRADES IN THE MARKETS IS A

SPECULATOR

THE GOVERNMENT SHOULD MAINTAIN A STRONG
CURRENCY THAT RETAINS A PAR VALUE WITH OTHER
STRONG CURRENCIES

In the late 1920's the stock market shot up into a bubble probably caused by excessive easy money or excessive money supply. The bubble turned into a crash in 1930 and a depression.

During the Great Depression , the Government produced a variety of policies hoping to improve the economy just as they are doing today. Did the Government involvement turn a recession into a depression?

In Japan in the late nineteen eighties the economy was starting to slow so the Government increased taxes and created a new consumption tax. The Japanese people were very much against it and the economy got worse. I believe the Japanese consumers were so irritated by the new consumption tax that they simply refused to spend. The government tried various programs and stimulus' to improve the economy but they did not reduce taxes. The Japanese people endured an economic slump called the lost decade. The much hated consumption tax was a main reason for Japan's lost decade. ANOTHER REASON WHY THE JAPANESE CONSUMERS ARE NOT BUYING IS BECAUSE THE VALUE OF THE CURRENCY IS TOO LOW, NOT BECAUSE THE INTEREST RATE IS TOO HIGH!

The Reagan administration and the Group of Seven decided to bash the dollar in 1986 and I believe this was the major contributor to the recession that began in the early 1990's. It may have also contributed to the 1987 black October.

It is my opinion that in the early 1990's the Mexican Government was told by some powerful world economists to bash the peso so they could export more. The peso did lose value. The result was a financial crisis by 1995. It appears to me that that is the only scenario that could have caused this result. The US survived the world financial crisis in 1998 because it had a strong currency. It is also my opinion that the International Monetary Fund or the World Bank or both were telling all the countries they were involved with to bash their currencies so that they could export more products. The result was weak currencies in those countries.

Another result was a world wide financial crisis that included all the countries the IMF or the World Bank were involved with.

These countries devalued their currencies. Today these same countries are thriving. That shows you how educational devaluation and reality can be.

Sure it possibly increased exports but what value was that? Since the exporters were not collecting the full value of their products due to a weaker currency, they were also exporting wealth . It lowered the standard of living in all those exporting countries.

The US, India, China and Japan were not involved in the 1998 financial crises because they were not influenced by the World Bank or the International Monetary Fund.

A strong US currency was the major contributor to the healthy US economy in the late 90's when much of the world was having a financial crises.

In the early 2000's the Government did not interfere in the bursting of the dot.com bubble or the recession that followed and there was no depression or financial crises. But the Government did start slashing interest rates and the value of the dollar started to fall. I believe that was a major contributor to the real estate bubble and the following financial crises that began after 2007.

THE BEST FINANCIAL REGULATION ANY GOVERNMENT CAN PRODUCE IS A STRONG, STABLE CURRENCY THAT RETAINS ITS PAR VALUE WITH OTHER STRONG CURRENCYS! The Federal Reserve does that by holding the interest rate high enough to keep the currency strong and to control the money supply. When interest rates are held high, money is more expensive to borrow and this reduces the amount of money moving into the economy. A reduced supply of money tends to increase the value of money. Excessively long periods of low interest rates tend to destroy the value of the currency.

WHAT WOULD HAPPEN IF AN ECONOMIC CRISES WAS ALLOWED TO RUN IT'S COURSE WITHOUT GOVERNMENT INTERFERENCE?

If the Government had not interfered in the economy in 2008 and let the "too big to fail" companies FAIL and had paid more attention to maintaining a strong dollar, by early 2009 most of the adjusting would have been achieved without Government help. The rest of the world would probably not have been involved. The companies that survived and the companies that emerged would have been much stronger and more competitive. The companies that survived would also have picked up the pieces of the failed companies. Everyone involved in the economy would have had a better idea of what was happening and confidence would have been much higher. It would have reduced monopolies and that would have been very beneficial to the economy and the society.

IF THE FED HAD CONCENTRATED ON MAINTAINING THE VALUE OF THE DOLLAR AS OPPOSED TO REDUCING THE VALUE OF THE DOLLAR IN 2000 IN ORDER TO INCREASE EXPORTS, WE VERY PROBABLY WOULD NOT HAVE HAD A HOUSING BUBBLE AND A WORLD ECONOMIC CRISES.

The Government should not bail out the poorest performing companies. The Government should do the opposite, protect the best performing companies from fallout caused by the miss management of the losers. Let the losers fall. Let the system self correct. That is called free market. That type of regulation won't do near as much damage to the confidence of the people as compared to Government interference.

Bailing out the weak companies with billions of taxpayer dollars is not fair to the strong companies or the taxpayers. It does more harm than good. It is also not free market.

History has proven that an economy where the people are more involved and the Government remains in the back ground is much more productive than when the Government plays a big roll. The Soviet Union is an example. In fact there are many examples. China, India and Northern Europe have all moved away from socialism and the results are obvious. That is why, in today's successful economies the smart Governments are reluctant to get too involved.

Of course the Government must use smart regulations to prevent the greedy from becoming too exuberant. Maintaining a strong , stable currency, using antitrust regulations to eliminate monopolies and regulating leverage are some examples of smart regulations.

The SOVIET UNION was a socialist type of governmental system. The Government took all the wealth from the wealth producers leaving no incentive to produce more wealth.

When the Soviet Union went broke it was because the wealth producers were not producing enough wealth to pay for all the Government subsidies. The Government did not let the wealth producers retain a fair share of the wealth as an incentive to produce more wealth.

This is a very important reason why societies, governments, economies go broke. And why socialism does not work. The wealth producers must be allowed to retain a fair share of the wealth they produce or they will quit producing and the system will go broke.

It appears the Keynesian economists of the world do not understand this. It appears the US Government does not understand.

The Soviet Union could have created phony wealth just like the US is doing now. They could have started up the printing presses and printed new money. It would not have done any good. They would still have gone broke. Because the money, the currency of a country is supposed to represent actual, real wealth, not phony wealth.

Is this the direction the US economy, the US financial system, the US society is headed?

## THE HEALTH INSURANCE BILL

This mandatory health insurance bill makes me feel for the first time in my life that I am being enslaved by my own Government. Basically, this mandatory health insurance bill, with the fines and jail time, is a form of slavery.

Of course people in the US government would never use the word slavery because slavery is unconstitutional.

This mandatory part is the worst part of the health bill. It is a major step toward taking away personal freedom. Believe it or not, slavery is the opposite of freedom.

Excessive taxation and other forms of mandatory transfer of wealth are incentives not to work. Definitely not the type of incentive a booming economy needs and definitely cannot be called a free market.

Will they socialize our society with mandates, taxes, regulations, fines, and fees that will take all the wealth away from the workers so that it can be distributed to those who don't want to support and care for themselves?

That is the same intent of socialism. The people who work are intended to carry the people who don't or won't work. The result is, nobody works. Why does it take so many years for a Government to figure that out?

Come on political experts, back off with the regulations, mandates and taxes that confiscate all the worker's wealth and allow the people the opportunity to help themselves. When you take away all the worker's wealth, which is their means of survival, you are setting the economy and society up for a major catastrophe.

Wealth producers need wealth to create wealth. Wealth producers must constantly create new wealth. And they must produce more wealth than they consume in order for an economy to grow. Churning and burning the old, existing wealth without creating new wealth is a guaranteed pathway for an economy to go broke. And that is exactly what Socialist countries do.

WEALTH

Grand domestic product and productivity gauges should be called wealth production gauges to remind society that constant production of new wealth is essential for the survival of any economy.

Wealth creation is very important for survival of an economy. Governments must treat it with respect. China, India, Russia, Germany and Brazil have all learned this the hard way, through Socialism. It seems India and Southern Europe and several South American countries have a learning problem.

Wealth must be produced by the wealth producers of a society. The more incentives they have to produce wealth, the more healthy a society or economy will be. Government must encourage and respect those incentives.

Over leveraging existing wealth should be restricted because it creates new, phony wealth where no real wealth exists. Real wealth can only be created by wealth producers sweat and creativity. That is why too many phony dollars representing a specific, restricted amount of existing wealth is inflationary. It does not matter who creates the phony wealth, the Government or independent institutions. PHONY WEALTH IS THE SAME AS PHONY MONEY. The creation of phony wealth is inflationary.

HOW TO TELL WHEN A CURRENCY IS INFLATED OR DEFLATED

When the value of the currency is at par with other strong currencies of the world, that means the currency represents the value of the true, real wealth of the society. When the currency of a country starts to lose its value compared to other strong currencies that means it is being inflated with phony currency.

The Government of a society should regulate its currency to maintain a continuous, constant value at par with other strong currencies. Then the currency will be the true value of the real wealth of its society. The Government should never allow it to be manipulated to benefit anyone.

Are bubbles examples of Governments creating and allowing creation of phony money? If creating phony money really worked it would have been put into practice a long time ago. If creating phony money worked no one would have to work.

The US Government has created trillions of dollars worth of this funny money with bailouts, stimulus activities, low interest rates and by buying back their own treasury bonds.

It appears the US Government has allowed private enterprise to create phony money with extreme leverage and low interest rates and no interest rates and creative loans and computer programs, reinsurance, derivatives, CDO's and excessive risk taking backed up by Government bailouts. I believe the whole insurance industry is a source of creation of phony money. I don't see where it creates real wealth in any form.

No wonder the financial institutions are showing obscene profits in this 2011 economy while the rest of the economy is producing minimal wealth.

Private enterprise is not legally supposed to create money. The Government is supposed to create money. But the responsibility of the Government is to create only money that is represented by real wealth that is created by the wealth producers of a society.

Now there is a massive excess of inflationary dollars that are not represented by real wealth being traded on currency exchange markets all over the world. The stock markets and real estate prices in the hot spots of the world are inflating because of the massive excess of dollars. World commodity prices are inflating because they are priced in these inflationary dollars.

The US massive creation of phony wealth is causing bubbles to form in the hot spots of the world. When the US economy starts to boom again that mass of excess dollars is going to come back and haunt the US society. Anyone like to see more bubbles or inflation?

LOW INTEREST RATES-HIGH UNEMPLOYMENT

The regulators are going to keep interest rates low because the unemployment rate is too high. But the unemployment rate is so high because the interest rates are so low.   When the US regulators try to use the interest rate to influence the unemployment rate, that is similar to the dreams of chasing rainbows.

The Federal Reserve claims that low interest rates will help people find jobs and lower the unemployment rate. But it is so obvious, the whole world can see that in the past few years (from 2006 to2012) the result has been the exact opposite of the Fed's claim. It is impossible to miss the reality. In fact it is more realistic to say lower interest rates caused the unemployment problem.

Keynesians say easy money causes growth in the economy. Just looking back at the financial policies the last few years in Europe and the US proves that they are wrong. In fact the complete opposite is true. The countries cannot spend more wealth than the society creates. The currency  must remain strong.

THE FED'S MANDATE  OF KEEPING INTEREST RATES LOW IN ORDER TO INCREASE EMPLOYMENT IS HAVING THE OPPOSITE EFFECT.

When the Government regulators are so reckless with the value of the currency they are being fool hardy, irresponsible and inconsiderate. In the case of the US dollar, the whole world suffers.

If the US  had not lowered interest rates so low and kept them so low for so long, the US would not have experienced such severe economic decline as has happened recently. In my opinion, if they had concentrated on maintaining the value of the currency, the world would have never experienced this financial crises.

In the late 1970's and early 1980's the dollar was in big trouble. Paul Volcer was put in as chairman of the federal reserve. He had to raise the interest rate up to 20% to bring back the dollar. After that the US economy started to boom. Then in 1986 the Group of Eight world powers decided the dollar was too strong and began to devalue it. In the late 80's the market crashed, black Monday. In the early 1990's the US was in recession.

In the  early 2000's the interest rate was brought down to near zero. The interest rates have been kept low and the US economy has been in trouble ever since.

Japan has kept its interest rates at zero or near zero for twenty years. It has experienced two lost decades as far as their economy is concerned.

If the US federal reserve would raise interest rates one quarter point or half a point now (November 2009), it would be a shock to the society. But if they raised the interest rate that amount now, without warning, and committed to bringing back the value of the dollar, after just a few days or weeks the US economy would start showing a very positive response. Commodity prices would start declining.

With an interest rate increase the economy would improve much faster than if the rates remain at zero. The reversal would send a strong message. An increase in interest rates would be the best jobs program the Government could possibly produce. I read someplace the Government has 47 jobs programs. None of them seem to work. Bring back the dollar.

Japan kept interest rates low for two decades. The Japanese are worried about deflation again. But what they are experiencing is not deflation. It is lack of demand. There is a big difference. The US was also worried about deflation recently. That was also not deflation, but simply a lack of demand. That is the same reason why we do not have price increases at this time. There is no demand. When the economy picks up and demand picks up, price increases will be back.

What the US and Japan both need to do is to raise the interest rate immediately, just enough to show both societies they are serious about protecting the value of the currency. Both economies would improve much more quickly than if the regulators continue to beat up the currencies by maintaining low interest rates.

The markets might initially fall, but when the economy starts responding with enthusiasm, the markets will come right back and keep on moving up as long as the economy keeps improving and as long as regulators concentrate on maintaining a strong currency as opposed to the other wild destinations they are seeking with their ridiculous low interest rates. Much of the markets rise has been due to smart money's expectation of inflation.

WEALTH PRODUCER

All the necessities of life. That is what we humans call wealth.

All value is produced by the wealth producer. Property has no value without a wealth producer's labor. Land is not worth anything without the wealth producer's labor creating a building or producing a crop or extracting the gold or oil. Ownership does not produce value. The labor of the wealth producer produces value. However, ownership through shrewd speculation can take advantage of changes in property value.

A wealth producer is anyone who in some way contributes to the production of wealth in a society. A society can create, produce or develop wealth only through a wealth producer. The wealth producer is the economic power of a nation. The wealth producer must be respected and encouraged by the Government. Wealth producers do not work for Government. Wealth producers work only in the private sector.

Examples of activities that do not produce wealth are Government spending that does not contribute to or improve wealth production.

The opposite of a wealth producer would be a wealth transfer recipient, the person on welfare or any person who does not contribute in some way to the production of wealth, that includes most Government employees. Everyone in a civilized society must have wealth to live, to exist. If a person is not producing the wealth he or she lives on then that person must be living on transferred wealth, other people's money.

FREE MARKKET! CREATING WEALTH IS THE KEY TO ECONOMIC GROWTH.

Governments do not produce wealth. They have no incentive to produce wealth. If governments need wealth they take it from the wealth producer. In order for an economy to grow, a wealth producer must produce more wealth than he or she consumes or spends, otherwise the wealth supply will shrink until there is no wealth left. That is why Socialism does not work.

That is why the Soviet Union went broke. A worker in the Soviet Union once said, "we pretend to work and the government pretends to pay us".

Some Government work programs have workers digging holes and then filling them back in. They say this adds to the grand national product. That is impossible. The only way to add to the GNP is for wealth producers to produce wealth. Some politicians believe that anything that puts people to work will improve the economy The economy will not improve unless the workers are producing real wealth. Hiring Government workers will not improve the economy.

If all jobs were that type of work the wealth supply would soon be gone. Workers must produce more wealth than it costs for them to do the work. Even infrastructure paid for by Government should help contribute to wealth production or it is wasted wealth. Spending on infrastructure has to have the potential to create wealth or assist in wealth production or it is wasteful spending. Digging a hole and then filling it back in does not produce wealth. It wastes or destroys wealth.

Government spending on social services can improve the economy if it frees up the workers (who would otherwise be caring for the needy) so that they can create wealth.

Of course Government spending on national security does not produce wealth but it is necessary in order to protect the wealth that has been produced and to protect the wealth producer.

Any person or business that creates more wealth than he or she or the business uses in the process of creating that wealth is a wealth producer. All personnel from management down to the janitor are wealth producers when they help the corporation or company or business produce more wealth than they are paid. If an industry does not produce more wealth than it consumes, then that industry is a parasite and the wealth producer has to carry it or it will go broke.

Government spending versus spending by the people; government, using other people's money, will build a bridge to nowhere and not even think of the value. But the people, using their own money, will not build the bridge if it does not offer value beyond its cost. If a bridge helps wealth producers get to their destination faster than without the bridge then the bridge has economic value and contributes to wealth creation.

But people also waste wealth. Should I spend or should I save? If you spend so much money on food that you gain excessive weight, you are wasting wealth because you are reducing your ability to produce wealth and you are increasing the possibility of higher medical costs. If you spend money to buy food that makes you healthier, you are increasing your ability to produce more wealth and you are spending wisely. If you save money until you can think of a way to spend it on something that will produce more money, then you are spending it wisely and you and the economy will benefit.

## HOW TO DESTROY AN ECONOMY

The ONLY way to grow an economy is for workers, entrepreneurs and businesses to produce and create wealth. What is wealth? Wealth is all the products, commodities, construction and other items produced by the workers, entrepreneurs and businesses that are demanded by the consumers.

Keynesians do not understand how necessary creation and production of wealth is in order for an economy to grow. The Keynesians believe the only way to grow an economy is through inflation. That is why they insist on 2% inflation and are much afraid of deflation. They do not seem to understand the absolute necessity of wealth in an economy. Wealth is the economy!

Inflation destroys an economy. Inflation reduces the value of the currency which represents the wealth in an economy. Since the value of the wealth remains constant, more units of the devalued currency will be needed to represent the given amount of wealth.

In today's economy some deflation would be healthy because the dollar is excessively inflated.

## THE CONSUMER IS 100% OF ANY ECONOMY

Only a human individual can decide to spend money. There is not an animal alive (other than humans) that can decide to spend money. No institution, corporation or business can decide to spend money. ALL MONEY TRANSACTIONS MUST BE DECIDED BY A HUMAN BEING!

Computers can be programmed to automatically spend money, but they must first be programmed by a human. No matter how complicated a transaction is, it must be decided by a human. When an individual human decides to spend money he or she becomes a consumer. Consumers are not 50% of the economy. They are not 60 or 70% of the economy. They are 100% of the economy.

A Government that wants a healthy economy must treat the consumer with utmost respect. That is one of the big reasons why a society needs a Government; to separate the real wealth from the phony money.

## TEMPORARY TAX CUTS

All temporary interference in an economy by a Government such as stimulus and temporary tax cuts do more harm than good because it burns wealth unnecessarily and causes confusion and interferes with long term planning. All stimulus packages, all temporary tax cuts and tax holidays do no good because all workers and businesses must plan long term. Everyone that has anything to do with a growing economy must have predictability.

George Bush's tax cuts were not as effective as previous tax cuts because they were temporary. Only permanent tax cuts are effective. That is why the recent extension of his tax cuts will also be disappointing.

## WE NEED SOME DEFLATION, LESS INFLATION

It appears that some economists believe that an economy can only produce wealth if there is a certain amount of inflation (for example 2% inflation). It seems that they also believe that deflation makes an economy weaker.

Currency represents the wealth of an economy. When the wealth of an economy remains constant an excessive amounts of units of the currency dilutes the value and makes the currency weaker, INFLATION. Inflation and deflation only represent the value of the currency of a society. Inflation means the value of the currency is shrinking. The currency is getting weaker. More of the currency must be handed over in order to buy a certain product.

Deflation means the currency is getting stronger. A shrinkage in the amount of units of the currency in circulation makes the currency stronger. There are fewer units of the currency to represent the given amount of wealth. DEFLATION. The whole world needs deflation to bring down the prices of commodities. We can thank the world currency wars for the high priced commodities.

Any political leader who wants to set up a socialist system is obviously extremely uninformed. Number one, you cannot have an economy without wealth producers producing wealth. Number two, wealth producers will not produce wealth without an incentive. The stronger the incentive, the more wealth produced. The weaker the incentive, the less wealth produced.

Without an incentive no wealth will be produced. Number three, the wealth producers will refuse to produce wealth if the wealth they produce is taken away and used to subsidize the lazy bums of the society.

In order for an economy to even exist, wealth must be created by wealth producers on a continuous basis. Socialist and dictators don't seem even to know what wealth is.

PANIC

## ALL THE WORLD'S ECONOMIC PROBLEMS ARE POLITICAL

I have not seen any proof that shows the society would have panicked if the Government regulators had not acted in 2007 and 2008. In fact I believe the regulators panic much easier than the people of the society and if the regulators had done nothing the recession would not have been nearly as severe. In the most severe economic downturns in US history, the depression of the 30's and the recent recession it was the regulators that panicked.

The only panic going on was the wobbly, uncertain regulations the regulators were handing down. When the regulators say the people would panic, I don't believe they have a clue what they are talking about. There is no way to prove that they are right. I believe the only purpose for such talk is to try to convince the society that they know what they are doing. Even in the situation of hyper inflation or any other financial crisis, I have never seen or heard of a society going into a panic, only regulators seem to panic.

## MARKETS GYRATE LIKE A HERD OF CLOWNS

The regulators, politicians and corporate management want to satisfy the markets. But the markets gyrate like a herd of clowns. They don't know what they want.

The managers, regulators and politicians should concentrate on what the consumers and workers and businesses want. When they satisfy this sector the economy will expand and improve and the markets will fall in line. Confidence will come back.

The Keynesians believe the only way to grow an economy is through inflation. That is why they insist on 2% inflation and are much afraid of deflation. But the truth is the only way to grow an economy is to create wealth. In today's economy deflation is healthy because of the excessively inflated dollar.

No economy should ever create phony money. An economy should only promote wealth production.

Socialism does not help anyone respect him or herself. Socialism trains everyone to become a pig at the trough.

Economics is not a number thing. Economics is a people thing.

## EQUALITY

Everyone has to be some place. You have just as much right to be here as I do. And I have just as much of a right to be here as you do. I am not any better than you, but I am just as good.

Some times we have to be reminded.

## GOVERNMENT WORKERS DO NOT PRODUCE WEALTH

Government workers do not produce wealth. The pay they receive is wealth produced by wealth producers in the private sector. The wealth producers must produce enough wealth to pay for themselves as well as enough wealth to pay the Government workers. The Government workers are carried by the wealth producers. That is the reality. Realistic economics still remains the exercise of the human species creating real wealth which is represented by a medium of exchange used by human consumers to consume.

## REASON WHY DEMOCRATS DO NOT UNDERSTAND ECONOMICS

The reason why most Democrats do not understand economics is because the majority of Democrats work in Government or institutions that do not produce wealth. They do not work in the private sector where the wealth is produced.

The people working in the private sector realize that they must help their employer produce wealth or their employer will go broke and they will be out of a job. Working in the private sector helps people understand economics. These workers tend to understand economics better than today's formally educated economists.

Economics is relatively simple. Today's economists tend to complicate economics much more than necessary with their computer models and mathematical equations.

Today's "economists" have complicated economics with "information overload" so much that nobody knows what real economics is all about.

Any human society that wants a successful economy must have wealth producers producing wealth. Without a society's medium of exchange or currency representing real wealth, the society cannot exist.

## SUBSIDIES

Subsidies and transfers of wealth such as bail outs and stimulus packages destroy economies because they do not increase the wealth in an economy. They destroy the wealth.

The only way for an economy to be healthy and strong is for workers to produce products and materials that are in demand by consumers.

And the market must be free from excessive taxes and regulations that drive up prices and reduce incentives to produce wealth. The market must be free of monopolies that destroy competition.

All temporary interference in an economy by a Government such as stimulus does more harm than good because it burns wealth unnecessarily and causes confusion. All stimulus packages, all temporary tax cuts and tax holidays do no good because all workers and businesses must plan long term. Everyone that has anything to do with a growing economy must have predictability.

All business planning is long term, that is why all tax cuts should be long term or permanent. One reason why the Bush tax cuts did not boost the economy is because they were not permanent tax cuts. Short term tax cuts are worthless as efforts to stimulate the economy.

## ENTREPRENEURSHIP AND OPPORTUNITY

Entrepreneurship is opportunity. Opportunity is entrepreneurship.

If Mr. Obama's goal of taxing wealth from the rich and subsidizing the less ambitious was in effect when Bill Gates created Microsoft or Steve Jobs created Apple we would not have Microsoft or Apple. They would not have had the resources or the opportunity to be so creative. None of the technological advances created in the 80's and 90's would have been created.

That is why Europe does not have any Bill Gates' or Steve Jobs'. The excessive taxes and regulations in Europe deprive the Bill Gates' and Steve Jobs' of the opportunity to be entrepreneurs.

## MONOPOLIES MAY BE CAPITOLISM, BUT THEY ARE NOT FREE MARKET

Monopolies are not free market. When monopolies are allowed

to form, the result is extreme distortion of the pricing system because the monopolies don't have any competition. They can control the supply, price and quality of the product. They will place extremely distorted prices on their products simply because they can, extreme markup pricing. That is especially the problem in the medical industry.

## THE CREATION OF HUMAN ECONOMIES.

The only thing that separates the human societies from the beasts of nature is that humans have developed a system that creates wealth and stores it in what we call currency. If the currency does not represent real wealth, if the currency is diluted and its value is reduced excessively by printing and creating phony money the economy will decline. With extreme devaluation societies will revert back to the days of the cave man. Money does not grow on trees. If it did, no one would have to work.

## SOCIAL GANGS, SOCIAL NETWORKS, SOCIAL GROUPS

A committee is a so called group of "experts" attempting to make the rules for a society. Government is depending more on "committees" all the time. They are attempting to make the rules for the "common good". Rules made in the best interest of everyone and the satisfaction of none. But a group of "experts", or the "committee", trying to make the rules is like a bunch of monkeys trying to play football. That is the definition of confusion.

The extreme right and extreme left are social gangs or groups where "committees of experts" make the rules and everyone in the gang follows those rules (similar to bees and ants). Socialism is another example of a social gang or group. Social Conservatism is another social gang. Is that where bipartisanship comes from?

DEMOCRACIES are ruled by the majority. Social gangs are organizations, organized to control Democracy. Organizations have power in a Democracy. The bigger the organization is, the more power it has.

Independents are in trouble! Independents refuse to organize. They are too independent. IT BOILS DOWN TO EITHER GROUP SELECTION OR INDIVIDUAL SELECTION. With group selection, the members of the group don't have a choice or the ability to make these choices, as with bees or ants. With individual selection, the individual has the choice and the ability to make these selections.

114

Would you rather be an ant, a bee or an individual? Everyone is an individual. No one is a group.

Everyone knows that the free market employer lays off the laziest employees first. And they retain the most productive workers. Are the majority of the hard core unemployed the laziest members of the labor force?

## GOVERNMENT HIPOCRACY

The Government takes away the money of the people and then tells the people if Government gives the money back to the people, the Government has a right to control the people or that the money the Government gives to the people belongs to the Government. The Government seems to believe that somehow through the confiscation transaction the money becomes the Government's money. Or does the Government believe all the money in the economy belongs to the Government in the first place? That is un-American, that is not freedom, that is slavery.

## DIET AND EXERCISE

Do you know why animals of the wild do not need a trillion dollar a year medical system? Because they go by natures rules. Who said that people were smarter than animals?

A lot of people die simply because they do not really want to live. If they really wanted to live they would take a lot better care of themselves. They could try some of nature's rules such as exercise and healthy eating.

If you eat and drink anything and everything, it does not matter how much you exercise, you won't lose weight. But if you eat and drink the right kind of food, you will lose weight, even if you don't exercise.

But exercise is very important for health reasons. The most important thing exercise does is strengthen the heart. As far as strengthening the heart is concerned, you don't have to kill yourself exercising.

You don't have to exercise strenuously for half an hour or more. Exercising just one minute a day, every day can start to strengthen the heart and also start an exercising habit It does not matter what type of exercise you do as long as it makes you breathe heavier than normal. Breathing heavier than normal means that the heart is working harder and strengthening. The heavier you are breathing, the harder your heart is working.

The most important thing is not to over work your heart. If you have not exercised for a long time, overworking your heart could be disastrous. You should check with your doctor before starting to exercise.

## EXERCISE / CHECK WITH YOUR DOCTOR

If you have not exercised for a long time it is very important that you check with your doctor to find out if any exercise will be too much for your heart. You will also want to know if there is any other reason why you should not exercise.

Also if you do a lot of exercise you should take at least two days off every week to let your heart catch up with all the work it has been doing all week.

But you do not have to kill yourself exercising. The most important thing is to get an exercising habit started. Exercising just one minute a day, every day is the easiest and best way to get a habit started.

If you feel weak, like you want to sleep, nauseous, like you want to throw up, dizzy, weak and wobbly, that could mean you have over worked your heart. You may also have unusual feelings in your chest in the middle of the night. Stop! Do not do any exercise for a while, until those feelings go away, maybe a day, maybe several days. If those feelings persist, see your doctor. It is serious. If you have not been exercising for a while it is easy to overwork your heart. So you do have to pay attention.

## YOU CAN STRENGTHEN YOUR HEART AND LIVE LONGER! YES YOU CAN!

### A FLEXIBLE CIRCULATORY SYSTEM

You probably have noticed that when you exercise, your veins become larger and more prominent. And the more you exercise the more prominent they become. That is because the heart has to pump more food and oxygen to the muscles. That is why exercise also strengthens the heart.

The veins and arteries have to get larger in order to transport the extra oxygen and food. That is what I call a flexible circulatory system. The flexibility of the arteries and veins prevents the dangerous build up of undesirable materials. Exercise can help keep your arteries and veins clean and clear.

116

EXERCISE CAN DEFEND AGAINST ALSHEIMER'S, DEMENTIA, PARKINSONS AND STROKE. YES IT CAN. It may even help reduce high blood pressure.

Exercising various muscles of the body causes the heart to work harder and blood vessels to expand and become larger because the muscles demand more blood. This exercise strengthens the heart and causes more blood flow throughout the whole body, including the brain. This sounds reasonable to me. What do you think? Try it, what do you have to lose?

The best exercise to strengthen the heart is walking because the leg muscles are the largest muscles of the body. I walk up to one mile every day. It definitely makes me feel better. I also do mild exercises such as calf lifts, squats and lifting weights. I don't overdo it. I just want to look and feel normal.

I am afraid not to exercise my body and brain. I am afraid if I do not exercise them I will lose them both and my longevity will be shortened. Your heart, your muscles, your brain, if you don't use it you will lose it. Walking may not develop leg muscles as much as some people would like. But it develops a strong heart and that is the most important thing in life.

MUSCLE POWER AND BRAIN POWER

Muscle power or brain power, if you don't use them you will lose them. No one is borne with brain power or muscle power. You have to work hard to acquire and maintain both of them. The harder you work at it the stronger they become, at any age.

Do you know why animals of the wild do not need a trillion dollar a year medical system? Because they go by natures rules. Who said that people are smarter than animals?

IS HEALTH CARE A BASIC RIGHT?

The subject of the right to the pursuit of happiness as stated in the Declaration of Independence, some people say that includes the right to health care.

In the Declaration of Independence the right to the pursuit of happiness means that the individual has the right to the pursuit of happiness so long as the individual does not victimize someone else. When someone victimizes another individual in the pursuit of his or her happiness then the victim is having his or her right to the pursuit of happiness infringed upon.

The right to the pursuit of happiness includes the right to pursue good health and to pursue wealth so long as some innocent individual is not being victimized. But when wealth is taken from someone who does not want to contribute that wealth and transferred to someone else to improve his or her health then the non consenting individual is being victimized. That was not intended in the Declaration of Independence.

No one has the right to victimize someone else for that person's benefit. That includes politicians and especially politicians. They do not have the right to select winners and losers. They do not have the right to victimize anyone, in this case victimizing them by confiscating their wealth, in order to pay for the medical expenses of someone else.

A CALORIE COUNTING DIET IS A STARVATION DIET
  1 protein = 4 calories
  1 gram carbohydrate = 4 calories
  1 gram fat = 9 calories
  1 gram alcohol = 7 calories
  I read a recent article, "Not all Calories Equal, Study Shows". They were trying to determine what calories cause weight gain and what calories don't. In other words they aren't sure what calories cause weight gain and what calories don't. Why would anyone join a calorie counting diet when no one knows which calories cause weight gain and which calories don't?

Calorie counting seems to ignore important things and emphasize unimportant things about food. For example, calorie counting tells you that meat has too many calories and ignores the value of protein in the diet. This makes it very difficult to find high protein foods, causing people to eat more low quality foods such as high carbohydrate foods.

A calorie counting diet is like a religion. A lot of people have faith in it. But the diet has some problems. One of the main problems is that it restricts consumption of high protein foods way too much. For one thing, high protein foods, such as fresh meats are much more filling and satisfying than high carbohydrate foods are. Therefore, if you eat a lot of protein you never feel hungry. I believe it is because high protein foods have much more food value.

Calorie counting seems more like a religion than a diet because it is so against eating meat. If you want to lose weight without feeling hungry you have to eat more meat, or at least more protein food of some kind. Many in our society are calorie counters. Could that possibly be why our society has an obesity problem?

In my experience, protein or animal fat do not cause you to gain weight, no matter how much meat you consume. I have been a heavy meat eater all of my long life. I only have a weight problem when I replace protein foods and green vegetables with carbohydrate foods. Carbohydrates such as foods made from grains, wheat, barley, corn etc. cause you to gain weight very rapidly.

The calorie counting diets are starvation diets. Since they restrict the amount of natural protein foods a person can eat, such as meat, they cause
people to either starve or eat high carbohydrate foods and junk foods. Unless you have a very strong will and can force yourself to constantly starve, you will gain weight if you are on a calorie counting diet or soon after you get off of one.

The reason why we have an obesity epidemic in the US is because the brilliant nutritionists are telling people not to eat meat. The overweight people are suffering from a shortage of protein in their diet.

The "expert" nutritionists are telling everyone they should be on a calorie counting diet. That is causing the obesity problem in the US. The calorie counting diet is actually a starvation diet and only the people with very strong will power can force themselves to stay on a starvation diet. They are the only ones capable of starving themselves for the rest of their lives. The reason why so many kids are becoming obese is because their parents have joined the calorie counting religion.

Pigs and cows get fat because they have a high carbohydrate diet, they do not eat meat. Carnivorous animals such as coyotes and lions don't get fat even though their main diet is meat, they do not eat carbohydrates. Animal fat and protein are not fattening. If they were, coyotes and lions would get fat. If they got fat they would not be able to hunt. They would not be able to survive. Nature has proven over thousands of years what is fattening and what is not.

Nature intended for humans to eat meat. Since life began on this planet, meat has been a main, reliable, healthy and dependable source of food and protein and I don't want to argue with nature. Nature did not intend for humans to eat excessive amounts of carbohydrates. And nature intended for humans to keep in good physical condition with exercise or physical work in order for the body to process the high protein meats.

The reason why I stress eating fresh meats rather than processed is because almost all processed meats have sugar added. I do not believe meat causes cancer. I believe sugar causes cancer. I eat a lot of well marbled, barbequed beef steak with salt and pepper seasoning only. For five years in a row I ate an average of 400 pounds of beef a year. You can eat all the meat you want and not gain weight. I have been a heavy meat eater all my life. I do not have a problem of gaining weight.

A high protein and low carbohydrate diet is the only way to lose weight and keep it off without starving.

There may be some problems with eating large amounts of meat. Excessive amounts of fats and oils seem to cause liver problems. I eat a lot of chicken thighs and legs, but I pull the skin off and trim the fat. I only eat pork about once a month because of the amount of fat in pork.

Also eating a lot of meat may tend to cause kidney stones. But carnivorous animals such as coyotes eat meat almost exclusively. They do not get kidney stones. But they run all day long.

I did develop kidney stones at one time in my life when I was not very active. After that I started walking on the tread mill up to mile a day. I did not reduce the amount of meat that I eat. I believe the walking agitates the materials in the bladder and keeps them from forming into kidney stones. It has been over five years since the kidney stone experience with no problems.

Jogging might be even better than walking because it applies more agitation to the materials in the bladder than walking.

THE PERSONAL PITY PROBLEM

Another cause of obesity is that some people, for one reason or another, feel sorry for themselves and give up on themselves and give up on life. The personal pity problem.

FARMER'S DIET

The farmer's diet is a high protein, high vitamin, very low carbohydrate diet. It does not cause you to starve or even be hungry. Because of the high protein content, the farmer's diet is a very satisfying diet. It will not cause you to crave high carbohydrate foods or junk foods.

It is called a farmer's diet because it consists of food grown on the farm, fresh meat, fruit and vegetables you have to process and prepare yourself. All of the high protein meats you want (even red meat). Farmers have been using the farmer diet for years. Farmers do not have a history of obesity.

You don't have to be a farmer to go on a farmer diet. You can buy all of the necessary fresh items at the local grocery store. I am constantly amazed at how well this diet works on many different health problems.

SUGAR CAUSES CANCER! YES IT DOES! Check it out. What have you got to lose?

Do you know why animals of the wild do not need a trillion dollar a year medical system? Because they go by natures rules. Who said that people are smarter than animals?

The medical industry has spent billions of dollars searching for a 'cure' for cancer. Since they have already spent billions of dollars searching for a cure, they are anxious to find that cure so that they can earn back some of that research money.

I doubt that the medical industry would be very happy if someone discovered the 'cause' of cancer and notified the society of that discovery. If society knew that some simple item was causing cancer and all they had to do was to eliminate that item and they would not get cancer or if they simply eliminated that item the cancer would go away, imagine how that would affect the medical industry.

If cancer suddenly became a rarity in society, the medical industry would not be able to earn back the billions of research money let alone a profit. They are searching for a cure. If they knew the cause of cancer I doubt if they would ever reveal that secret.

With this thought in mind do you think the researcher who discovers the cause of cancer will ever let society know about the discovery and thereby lose the opportunity to recover the research money and also lose the chance to make a profit? Very unlikely! If we want to know the cause of cancer we will have to discover it ourselves

CANCER FIGHT

I had a brother die of cancer. We were both teenagers. I did not like the idea of dying of cancer so I started searching for the cause of

121

cancer.

I am not a doctor! Before you try any of these ideas, you should first check with your doctor. I am also not a scientist. I'm just a western hick. I have never been back east where all the "experts" live.

My brother who died had a major sweet tooth. He was never overweight. After our family realized he had a problem our mother started baking many sweet confections. She knew he liked them and she tried to make him as happy as possible. We all liked them and we had no clue sugar could be a problem.

Ever since my brother died I have been looking for causes of cancer. After several years of various observations, I became convinced that sugar had something to do with cancer.

About forty years ago I developed a problem of food pushing up between two molars and up into my nose cavity. A dentist had recently installed a filling in one of the molars. He became highly irritated that I would suggest that the filling was causing the problem. I never went back to a dentist. I simply chewed on one side of my mouth. But occasionally food would still push up into my nose cavity.

After a while a clear fluid began to drain out of my nostril. I became concerned that it might develop into cancer. At the time I was eating my share of sweets. I cut out my sugar consumption as much as possible. The drainage out of my nostril stopped. But I found it is very difficult to stop eating sugar. Soon the drainage started up again.

I became obsessed with controlling my sugar consumption. I found that I could control the drainage simply by controlling my sugar consumption. I developed a diet of meat and green vegetables. I bought fresh meat and vegetables and processed all my own food to make sure no sugar was added. It worked. As long as I was on that diet there was no drainage.

But I was not getting enough to eat and I would go out and eat at a restaurant or eat a pizza or some other tasty meal. The drainage would come right back. I would stop eating sugar and go on my sugar free diet and within two or three days the drainage would go away. But when I ate something with sugar, within a day or two the draining would come back. I would go back on my sugar free diet and within a matter of two or three days the drainage would go away again.

I finally had the cavity taken care of and the drainage stopped. But I have had several other symptoms of cancer come and go over the years. I would think that the problem was solved and I would eat something with sugar. The problem would come right back. I would go back to my strict cancer fighting diet and the problem would go away. For over forty years now, I have been doing this routine. It works every time.

If I had gone to a doctor they would have sliced and diced, radiated and chemo-therapied me to death. Not to mention all of the expensive chemicals they would have told me I had to take. Don't tell anybody but I have not spent a dime on cancer treatment.

If I had not discovered how destructive sugar in the system was, I believe I would have been dead of cancer a long time ago. I am constantly amazed at how well this diet works on many different health problems.

I have kept myself in good physical condition all of my life. I believe that is also important in fighting cancer.

## MY CANCER FIGHTING DIET
I use an eight quart crock pot. I put in one and one half quarts of water and three cups of black beans. I let the beans cook for four hours on high.

After I get the beans cooking, I start chopping five pounds of chicken into the pot with the beans. I chop the chicken in approximately one half inch squares. The chicken should cook for at least two hours with the beans.

At the end of the four hour cooking of the chicken and beans, I add the green vegetables. I let them cook with the chicken and beans for another 25 minutes to half hour. Three green bell peppers chopped, (no colored vegetables, colored vegetables are too sweet), three cups broccoli chopped, four cups celery chopped, 10 to16 ounces of spinach chopped.

At the end of the cooking, I unplug the crock pot and add one teaspoon coarse ground black pepper and six teaspoons salt. I pour it into a container with cover and let cool. Then I put in the refrigerator. That is my breakfast for the next seven days.

For the other two meals I barbeque beef steak, pork steak or chicken thighs or drumsticks with salt and pepper seasoning, (eggs and fish are also ok in this diet). I barbeque year round.

## SUGAR CAUSES CANCER (continued)
I have been a meat eater all my life. I probably eat more meat

than anyone in the world. Well marbled beef is my favorite. I don't believe the 'expert's theory that red meat causes cancer. I have been eating well marbled barbequed beef as a main part of my cancer fighting diet for more than forty years.

In my experience beef definitely does not cause cancer. For five years in a row I ate about 400 pounds of beef a year; a barbecued steak almost every day, year round. The only seasoning I use is salt and pepper, no sauces or rubs of any kind because most of those have sugar added. I buy all my food fresh and prepare it myself. I don't take any medications, pills, cold remedies, not even aspirin. Many medicines have sugar in them to make them taste better.

Eating a lot of meat can cause kidney stones to form but a lot of walking or jogging can keep kidney stones from forming. I try to walk up to a mile a day. It definitely works for me.

I definitely attempt to eliminate sugar in anything I eat. Eliminating sugar in my diet is my major cancer fighting goal. You would be surprised how difficult eliminating sugar in your diet is. It seems every processed food has sugar added. I find it impossible to find any processed, packaged meat that does not have some type of sugar added. Almost all canned goods have sugar added. Almost all breakfast foods have sugar added. I do not eat any sweet fruit of any kind.

I have heard people say for many years that red meat, especially beef causes cancer. Almost nobody eats meat, including red meat, without some type of sauce, rub or special seasoning, all of which have sugar in them. Almost all processed meats have sugar added.

That is where I think the surveys go wrong. I think it is the sugar, not the red meat that causes cancer. I eat other popular, fresh meats, barbecued, roasted and fried. I use only salt, pepper and, sometimes, garlic, no other seasoning or sauces. I believe most special seasonings, rubs and sauces have sugar added even if it doesn't says so on the label. I never eat any processed meats.

Your body knows how much water you need to drink, much better than the 'experts'. If you are thirsty, drink water. That is all I ever drink is water. I like to keep it simple. Plus I stay away from sugar or alcohol or caffeine. I never allow nicotine in my system.

Oxygen is the most important element in the body's defense system's fight against sickness, viruses, cancer and many other irritations that come along.

It takes a lot of oxygen for the body to burn up the energy foods.

It is my opinion that stimulant  type energy foods like sugar, caffeine, alcohol and tobacco's nicotine rob the blood of the oxygen that the body's defense system needs to fight all health problems.  With the reduced oxygen supply, the body's defense system cannot do its job.

People who eat a lot of sweets have excess sugar in the blood and the excess sugar weakens the body's defense system because it burns up the oxygen supply.  If you eliminate sugar, alcohol and caffeine from your diet and tobacco from your habits, you will be surprised at how much healthier you become and how much better you feel.

When excessive sugar lingers in the blood it is fought by the body's defense system.  This runs down the body's normal defense system and allows various viruses and bacteria to survive unchecked in the body.  Excessive sugar that lingers in the blood stream appears to be treated as a toxin or poison by the defense system of the body.

One way the body reduces sugar in the blood is through exercise. The extra heavy breathing also increases the oxygen supply in the blood stream.  Exercise also strengthens the heart muscle making the individual more capable of surviving shocking traumatic experiences, increases blood circulation and helps eliminate impurities through sweating.  The stronger heart helps blood circulation to all the body's senses and the brain.  A strong heart increases the size of arteries, veins and capillaries improving circulation and possibly reducing clogged arteries.

An active body would have less blood sugar and therefore be less apt to develop cancer.  And an active body would possibly help reduce an existing cancer.

I believe there are several defense procedures the body uses to reduce the sugar in the  blood.  In some people who eat excessively sweet foods, the body adapts after a period of time.  The body sets up a defense procedure that changes the excess sugar in the blood into fat immediately.  The sugar does not linger in the blood and the person becomes overweight very quickly.  With the excess sugar out of the blood, the defense system would remain healthy.

In this situation, the excessively overweight person would be less apt to develop  cancer than a slender person.  This defense activity would usually be found in a person who started on a heavy sugar diet in very early childhood.  In this situation the amount of sugar in the blood can be higher in an underweight person than in an overweight person. But I believe, over a period of time, this defensive process can appear or disappear, depending on diet, in a person of any age.

One type of defense mechanism the body has against excessive sugar lingering in the blood is exhibited as acne. The defense mechanism removes the excess sugar in the blood through the pores in the skin, a process often resulting in pimples or acne. People who have acne should have a lower amount of sugar in the blood and therefore be less apt to develop cancer. This defense mechanism would be found in people who started a heavy sugar diet in childhood. It is also possible that exercise will reduce the acne problem.

In people who are not used to eating sweets and who then suddenly develop a sweet tooth, the defense mechanism does not have time to develop. Sugar lingers longer in the blood of such a person. This type of person would have high blood sugar and be most apt to develop cancer.

An example of this type of person would be a person moving from a country of low sugar consumption to a country of high sugar consumption and developing a sweet tooth. Another example of this type of person would be someone who grew up in a family with low sugar diet and, after leaving home, developed a sweet tooth.

When excessive sugar lingers in the blood it is fought by the body's defense system. This runs down the body's normal defense system and allows various viruses and bacteria to survive unchecked in the body. Excessive sugar that lingers in the blood stream appears to be treated as a toxin or poison by the various defense systems of the body.

Cancer is not caused by smoke in the lungs, by various weed sprays or by asbestos. But these irritants work as catalysts to help start cancer. Persistent bruising or irritation of various organs of the body such as ulcers in the stomach or food being pressed between the teeth and into the gums and jaw also work as catalysts to help start cancer. Many other examples of persistent irritation to various parts of the body can be found. A highly tense or nervous person who seems constantly to have a lump in his or her throat would be a catalyst that could someday turn into cancer.

But when a certain part of the body is constantly irritated, as in the case of an ulcer in the stomach or smoke in the lungs and the defense system is run down because of fighting excess sugar in the blood, these added stresses overtax the defense system. At the area of irritation, normal cell division is interrupted. Possibly the excess sugar in the blood causes a coating to form over the cell wall which then causes an interruption in the complicated message transfer necessary for normal cell growth. As a result, abnormal and possibly cancerous growth might begin.

When the body is free of the various external irritations that can help start cancer and there is excess sugar in the blood, the excess sugar causes the defense system to deteriorate and a condition called leukemia occurs. We often see this situation develop in young people who have not had time to develop irritating habits such as smoking.

It seems that once a cancerous growth has advanced to the serious stage and the defense system seems to have been excessively run down, sugar consumption has to be reduced to as near zero as possible. Even a small amount of sugar seems to keep the cancer active. But if the person goes on a strict "no sugar" diet, the defense system seems to improve almost immediately and within a matter of days the cancer seems to be on the run. But if the person eats something as simple as one apple or drinks one alcoholic or sweet beverage, the cancerous activity seems to come right back.

The average blood transfusion does not help a cancer victim. Blood from a person on an average US diet would probably have too much sugar in it. But, I believe, a transfusion of blood from a person on a sugarless diet would improve a cancer victim's condition almost instantly.

Of course, everyone needs a certain amount of sugar in his or her system. But I have had doctors tell me that the meat and the vegetables that I eat give me all the sugar I need. A person on a low sugar or no sugar diet will have the minimum amount of blood sugar the body requires.

Sometimes, when the blood sugar gets too low, a person will develop dizziness or possibly even low blood pressure. These problems require an appointment with your doctor.

The following is what I have found out about foods and what I have decided to include in and exclude from my diet. I have found it best and safest to process and cook all my own food so I can be sure no sugar has been added.

Restaurant eating is risky. Many restaurant foods have sugar added, as in breading batters used for shrimp and deep fried onion rings. Almost all breads, buns and biscuits have sugar added. Sugar is added in soups and stews, even sea food stews. Almost all salad dressings and steak sauces and catsup have sugar added. French fries and potato chips have a sugar solution sprayed on them during processing for coloring and taste purposes. Canned vegetables contain sugar to maintain color and give flavor. In fact, almost all canned foods have sugar added even if it does not always say so on the label. Most processed meats such as ham, lunch meats, hot dogs, sausage and bacon contain sugar. Store bought bread and pastries all have sugar added.

Trying to eliminate sugar in a diet is so difficult that I have developed a simple diet that I have used for over forty years. Over the years I have strayed from this diet many times. Every time I ate something such as a piece of pie or an apple or ate at a restaurant, the cancer symptoms would reappear almost instantly as within a day or two. But when I immediately went back to my basic cancer fighting diet, (sugar free diet) the cancer symptoms would disappear within three or four days.

I believe that we should eat no artificial sweeteners and drink absolutely no alcoholic beverages, especially wine. We should also avoid soft drinks such as cola, diet drinks , fruit juices, fruits (even when dried), citrus fruit, or berries. All I drink is water.

We should also avoid maple, boysenberry and corn syrups. We should watch for different forms of sugars noted on labels. Dextrose, fructose, sucrose, lactose are all forms of sugar and all should be avoided. Honey or products sweetened with honey are no better than products using sugar.

Almost all processed breakfast cereals contain sugar. There are a few that do not such as oatmeal, puffed rice or puffed wheat. But even these cereals often have sugar added. We should not chew gum or eat candy, ice cream, sherbet or any other sweetened desert, even if they are sweetened with artificial sweeteners or honey.

Foods I am not sure about as far as being sweet enough to cause cancer are vinegar, carrots, potatoes and sweet corn.

When I quit eating sugar, I quit seeing the dentist. I am not recommending that you stop seeing your dentist. I did not go to a dentist for twelve years. But I did brush my teeth every morning.

After twelve years I went to the dentist to replace a faulty filling that caused food to press up between my teeth and into my jaw and nose cavity. I had my teeth checked and found that I had no cavities. I believe not eating sugar kept me from developing cavities and other tooth problems.

It was this dental ailment, food pressing between my teeth and up into my jaw and nose that helped me form these opinions of cancer. When I did eat sugar (it usually was not much and was by accident in a restaurant, since I was trying to keep from eating it,) a clear fluid would drain out of my nostril. At the same time, other sores that I happened to have would heal very slowly.

Then I would watch my diet closer and not eat sugar at all. The draining out of my nostril would stop and the sores would start healing again. I subjected my body to this unpleasant process, sometimes on purpose, numerous times.

When I went to the dentist the first time in twelve years, I also had him fix the faulty filling. Food no longer presses between my teeth and up into my jaw and nose. I am healing now but I still cannot eat sugar or the irritation and draining comes back.

I firmly believe that sugar causes cancer and that I actually had cancer in the past, a cancer that I was able to turn on and off, depending on diet. I believe I would be dead of cancer today if I had not developed this theory on cancer.

I did not go to a doctor about my suspicions that I had cancer because doctors are extremely expensive. I could not afford the expense and I seemed to have everything under control anyway.

I believe my theory will work with almost all types of cancer. We will also have some other very pleasant surprises in our lives when we quit eating sugar. The absence of excess sugar in the blood seems to allow the defense system and the antibodies to build up so that we almost never catch a cold or any other type of virus infection. If we do catch a virus, it seems to affect the body only mildly.

Avoiding sugar will virtually eliminate tooth decay, not to mention helping to keep a trim body. That is why animals of the wild do not need a dentist. They do not eat sugar.

I further believe this sugarless diet will affect other serious illnesses in a very positive way. I believe if a person on this sugarless diet acquires one of the fevers brought on by insect bite, such as malaria, spotted fever, sleeping sickness, bubonic plague, he or she will have much milder symptoms than a person who is on a heavy sugar diet.

I also believe this sugarless diet will cause various infections to be less severe than they would otherwise be. Wounds and infections will heal much faster than they otherwise would.

This sugarless diet may be applicable to the AIDS problem. It is a known fact that when the AIDS virus first invades a body the body's defense system puts up a tremendous fight and nearly eliminates the virus. But then the defense system weakens and the virus takes over. Possibly, if the body's defense system was not weakened by excessive sugar intake it may be able to totally eliminate the virus.

Even if a person does not have cancer, going on this sugarless diet may improve his or her chances of living longer simply because he or she would be healthier and more resistant to infection and disease. Also a healthier person could reasonably expect to save  money by reducing medical expenses.

Many people eat for entertainment. I used to, but I don't any more. I eat for food value. A person does not need a variety of food. A person can live a very healthy life by eating vegetables, and something for protein and drinking a lot of water.

Keeping in good shape physically is very important, a lot of walking if possible. Because they eat for entertainment as opposed to eating strictly for nutrition, the US citizens are eating themselves into an early grave and giving their wealth to the medical industry along the way

If everyone in the US went on a diet without sugar, caffeine, alcohol or nicotine  the US would become the healthiest society in the world. The medical industry would be screaming because no one was getting sick.

Even people who had been sick would very probably become healthy because the body is an amazing, self healing machine. Every sickness caused by bacteria and virus from the common cold to, possibly, AIDS would fade into distant memory. I am constantly amazed at how well this diet works on many different health problems.

You know, it truly is amazing how fast a body will heal itself of almost any kind of sickness or problem on a strict diet like this. It must be the way nature intended for the human being to eat. It appears asparagus, broccoli, celery, green beans, spinach, green bell peppers, avocados, almost any green vegetable that is not too sweet (green peas may be too sweet) will work, and high protein fresh meats and eggs to eat and water to drink. No deviation from this diet until the body has healed. Then it is possible a person could go back to eating crazy again.

FATHER NATURE

Mother nature has wimped out with her compassionism and excessive kindness, excessive nurturing, networking, multitasking and political correctness.

Let's try Father Nature for a while. Let's try tough love. Let's try reality. Sometimes tough love is not compassionate or fair or kind. But it is reality. Nature intended for all mammals to be self supporting. The world does not owe anyone a living. Everyone has to work for a living.

Nature is not fair. Good luck and bad luck are much more common than fairness in nature. That is why you have a brain, to steer yourself to the lucky side as opposed to the unlucky side.

Nature intended for all hardships, mistakes, challenges to be educational, all risks to be rewarded. Good risks and poor risks to be rewarded in kind.

Nature is going to constantly give you challenges. That is what you have a brain for, to answer those challenges. That is why you feel so good when you conquer those challenges. Because that is what nature intended. And that is also why you feel so bad when you give up.

In the beginning, all creatures lived off natural resources. And they still do! Since the beginning of oxygen breathing life, nature's laws have never changed.

If no one is willing to work and sweat to mine and refine all the natural resources and grow food and build shelters, a human society cannot exist.

All of the people who are willing to work and sweat to mine, refine and process all the products of wealth I call wealth producers. The wealth created by these wealth producers is the economy. Without these wealth producers there is no economy. Without an economy a human society cannot exist.

This is where socialists of the world have a problem. You can talk about compassion and nurturing all you want but without an economy a human society cannot exist. Nature intended for every creature to support him or herself.

Everyone has to support him or herself by being a wealth producer. Nature never intended for anyone to get a free ride. There are examples all over the world today that prove socialism does not work.

NATURE'S FREEDOM

You find a bird that has a broken wing. You take it in and help it heal. When you think it is strong enough you let it go. You would

131

like to keep it but you know it wants to go and you love it. If it comes back that is fine, but most of them will never come back. Because freedom is much more important than security.

That is why the strong, the brave and the wise do not have faith in religion. Because nature's freedom is much more important than security.

**This is just my opinion but I believe all medicines, which are nothing more than chemicals, destroy the body's natural defense system.**


ENVIRONMENTAL

PLAYING WITH FIRE

Once upon a time, not too many years ago in universal speak, there was a planet, not our beautiful green earth but it was a lot like earth. It had a beautiful green surface of oxygen generating plant life.

The oxygen generated by this plant life also created and maintained an ozone layer in the planet's atmosphere.

This ozone layer protected the planet from the hostile solar rays that causes all other planets of the universe to be hostile to living, oxygen breathing creatures. This is the same solar hostility that causes all other planets of the universe to be uninhabitable waste land whipped by severe solar winds and scorched by solar rays.

The ozone layer was the unique bubble of life for this planet.

The planet had existed for millions of years and evolved to the point where there were all manner of living, oxygen breathing creatures. Even human type creatures.

There was also abundant supplies of oxygen containing water. There were continents and oceans. The weather was mild with general rainfall falling on many areas of the planet.

The mild weather and rainfall was essential for the existence of the green plant life that produced the ozone layer, the unique bubble of life.

If the green plant life disappeared, for whatever reason, the unique bubble of life would also disappear.

But the uninformed human like creatures persistently depleted the green plant life using ancient trees for wood and clearing and burning forests for personal reasons. With unforgivable selfishness they harvested the forests, they chopped and burned the ancient tropical rain forests.

In a relatively short period of time in universal speak, the plant life began to disappear. The oxygen supply of the planet began to decrease.

Holes in the bubble of life, the atmosphere's ozone layer began to appear allowing hostile solar rays to heat up the oceans and cause the mild weather conditions to become more and more severe.

There was less general rainfall because the moisture was concentrated in the severe storms that caused droughts. The dry weather allowed wild fires and forest fires to burn uncontrolled. The deserts became larger.

When the human like species realized what was happening they began to furiously build dams and canals and started huge planting campaigns, trying to reverse the trend. But it was too late. The ancient forests could not be replaced in time.

The condition began to feed upon itself. The solar rays began to cause extremely fast evaporation of the water of the ocean and began to burn up the remaining oxygen. The fast evaporation caused extreme weather changes. Hurricanes became common. Flooding washed out plant life. Winds of over 200 miles per hour stripped foliage from the remaining plant life.

With no green plant life the carbon dioxide was not regenerated back into life supporting oxygen.

Oxygen became more and more scarce. Oxygen was also a major defense against germs, bacteria and viruses. Epidemics of various diseases wiped out large numbers of oxygen breathing creatures. The remainder died a short time later because there was not enough oxygen in the air to support life.

In a very short period of time in universal speak the planet became just another brown planet of the hostile universe. The planet was Mars.

Are we playing with fire?

Have there been several other planets over the history of the universe that were very similar to earth?

Is the reason why we never find other planets trying to

communicate with us because the humans have always destroyed themselves leaving no one to communicate with?

Does it always signal the end of this type of planet when the human species over populates and over exploits?

Activities in the universe as compared to activities on our planet earth are extremely unfeeling and severely hostile to all forms of life. There is no compassion. There is no second chance.

## DESTRUCTION OF FORESTS

More than 80% of the world's forests have been totally eliminated over the past 150 years. That is a shocking reduction in the oxygen generating plant life.

The remaining forests will disappear much faster now because there is much more demand than supply. There is more demand now than there has ever been in the history of our world due to overpopulation by the human species.

Green plants use carbon dioxide like humans use oxygen. Carbon dioxide is as important to plant life as oxygen is to human life. They turn carbon into fibers for their skeleton, structure and form. They release the oxygen into the air for ozone to protect us from the hostilities of the universe and release oxygen for us to breathe. The oxygen that is locked up in carbon dioxide cannot be used for breathing purposes. Plant life has to first release the oxygen from the carbon dioxide. Of course humans produce much more carbon dioxide than the world plant life can use. Even if the plant life that existed 150 years ago existed today there would be much more carbon dioxide than the plant life could use up. .

Over the South Atlantic Ocean in the past ten years there has been a continuous huge blanket of smoke covering an area with a diameter about 2000 miles across. This huge blanket of smoke is caused by the burning of rainforests in Africa and South America. In Indonesia the smoke from burning rain forests is so thick it is a threat to life. It has been this way for several years. The smoke is spreading across much of Asia.

We must stop all destruction of all forests any way we can and start planting new growth as fast as we can. We should be planting trees and spreading tree seeds all over the world in an attempt to replace those trees that have been eliminated.

If the humans had replaced the billions of trees as they used them, that eighty percent of forests that were totally eradicated would still be on earth. There would be billions more trees on our earth today. There would be less excess of carbon dioxide today because those billions of trees would have used the carbon for structure and released the oxygen into the air. And there would be less threat of holes in the ozone layer because the trapped oxygen in the carbon dioxide would have been released to create ozone.

It is very possible that in the next few years things will start getting worse fast. The remaining forests are being destroyed faster today than ever before in the history of our world due to the demands of over population by the human species.

## OUR OXYGEN SUPPLY IS GETTING DANGEROUSLY LOW

The oxygen in the air we breathe has decreased by almost half in recent years. Scientist have discovered that at one time the earth's air consisted of 38%oxygen. Today the air we breathe contains no more than 19 to 21% oxygen at the highest and in some areas as low as 11 to 13%. Oxygen breathing creatures cannot exist on less than 7% oxygen in the air.

When oxygen in the air diminishes another very important resource also starts to disappear, $H_2O$, water. A big part of water is made up of oxygen.

Oxygen plays a very important role in the healing process and defense against disease of all oxygen breathing creatures. Oxygen defends the body against germs, bacteria and viruses. The most important element in the body's natural defense system is oxygen.

In the southern hemisphere in 1997 approximately 1200 young sea lions died from a virus infection. It is possible that low oxygen levels in the air they were breathing contributed to their huge losses.

If the percentage of oxygen in the air we breathe gets much lower, is it possible that a tree could become more valuable than a human life? The human species must become much more aggressive in the preservation of the world's forests.

## OZONE AND EL NINOS

El Ninos are unusually warm ocean currents. Very probably some of these unusually warm currents are caused by the solar rays coming through the holes in the ozone layer. Do the solar rays penetrating the ozone layer and reaching the earth's surface overheat the oceans? Does this penetration cause the unusual weather conditions that are happening in our world?

In mid September 1997 hurricane Linda off the coast of Baha California had winds of up to 215 miles per hour. It is suspected this hurricane was caused by an unusual El Nino in the pacific Ocean.

Ozone is made up of oxygen and nothing else. In chemistry the symbol of ozone is "O3", with three oxygen molecules instead of the normal two. It is generated by an electrical discharge in ordinary air.

This ozone layer protects our planet from the hostile solar rays that cause all other planets of the universe to be hostile to living, oxygen breathing creatures. This is the same solar hostility that causes all other planets of the universe to be uninhabitable waste land whipped by severe solar winds and scorched by solar rays.

The solar rays that penetrate to the earth's surface also burn up much of our valuable oxygen.

The ozone layer is the unique bubble of life for this planet. As the ozone layer diminishes the moderating effect the ozone layer has on our climate will also diminish. The solar hostilities will have more and more influence on our planet's weather. Days will become hotter and nights will become cooler. The hot spots of our planet will become hotter and the cold spots will become colder. Storms will become more severe.

On a day in July 1998 the hottest temperature in the world was 129 degrees above in Death Valley California and the coldest temperature in the world was 103 degrees below in Antarctica, a difference of 232 degrees. The average temperature may not change much but this difference will get larger and larger and the ozone layer diminishes.

As the temperatures become more and more extreme there will be more stormy weather and the storms will become more severe. There will be more wind on the earth and the wind velocity will increase. Storms will have more violent and erratic gusts.

Depletion of the ozone layer means the climate will not only get warmer, but will also get colder than normal. This means storms will become much more severe.

Due to global warming, moisture distribution on the earth's surface will be more and more concentrated in flooding and drought conditions. Severe storms will concentrate the moisture in relatively small areas, leaving less moisture to be distributed over the rest of the planet. It will not be good for crop production.

The southern hemisphere of the earth has less land surface than the northern hemisphere and therefore less oxygen producing plant life. That is why the rain forests are so vital to the southern hemisphere and why the ozone layer in the southern hemisphere is disappearing first.

In October 1998, the hole in the ozone layer over the south pole expanded to 10 million square miles. The hole is beginning to expand extremely fast. Now there are also holes appearing in the ozone layer over Russia and the north pole.

We must educate the people who live in and destroy rain forests of the extremely vital importance of the rain forests. We must stop all destruction of all forests any way we can and start planting new growth as fast as we can. We must convince governments to stop business concerns from destroying the remaining forests. These things should have been done yesterday.

We must start working on them today like there was no tomorrow. Because if we don't there won't be.

CARBON DIOXIDE

The ozone layer protects our little green planet from the extreme heat and extreme cold of the universe.

The average temperature of the world may not be changing much but the receding ozone layer is allowing the more extreme heat and extreme cold in the universe to reach the earth's surface. The cold temperatures are getting colder and the hot temperatures are getting hotter due to the shrinking ozone layer. These colder and hotter than normal temperatures are causing much more violent weather conditions than the world has seen in the past. These violent weather conditions could change our unique little green planet into a brown planet.

The industrial world does tend to produce too much carbon dioxide. This excess carbon dioxide is locking up the oxygen in our atmosphere. This loss of oxygen is causing the depletion in the ozone layer (ozone is made up of oxygen) that protects us from the extreme heat and cold of the universe.

The holes are caused by a shortage of oxygen. Ozone is oxygen. The nearly exclusive generator of oxygen on our planet is green plant life. Green plants use carbon dioxide like people use oxygen. They turn the carbon into fibers for their skeleton, structure and form. They release the oxygen into the air for ozone to protect us from the hostilities of the universe and oxygen for us to breath. The extreme decrease in the green plant life of our world is contributing to the excess carbon dioxide in the atmosphere.

Since plant life uses carbon dioxide and changes the carbon into fibers and returns the oxygen into the atmosphere, increasing plant life would increase oxygen and ozone in the air and also reduce the amount of carbon dioxide in the atmosphere.

## SUPER HUMAN THEORY

Some religious people believe their God created the world in seven days and seven nights. And their God would never allow anything to happen to their world. That is why they do not believe in global warming. But they also do not believe in birth control and that is causing over population of humans to destroy their and our world. Some day that is going to cause weeping and gnashing of teeth.

This extremely dangerous attitude is a very real threat to our unique little green planet. This attitude is the main reason why our world is so over populated by humans today. We can and must work around this dangerous attitude.

The believers of this theory do not believe there are holes in the ozone layer. They do not believe there is any threat what so ever.

But those of us who live in the real world know better. We know that extremely powerful forces in the universe would snuff out our little green planet in a nanosecond if it gets in the way of the tremendous fireworks. We know that the powerful forces in the universe do not have compassion or sympathy or kindness or fairness. We know that to those powerful forces the lives of oxygen breathing creatures mean absolutely nothing. We know that the human species can destroy this planet and we hope that the human species can also save this planet. We also know that our unique little planet is a near freak of the universe. We know there is no other planet like ours in our immediate vicinity of the universe.

We must get the attention of the rest of us who live in the real world and begin to do things now.

I don't believe the world was created in seven days and nights. I believe the world was created over many millions of years and the global warming is real. I believe the over population of the human species is destroying our world in, maybe not seven days and nights, but in a very short period and the whole world should start practicing birth control like there was no tomorrow.

The world and all of nature's human societies are being destroyed by the over population of humans with their selfish, greedy demands. The best and probably only way to stabilize the world's climate change problem is for humans to use birth control.

There are many people who believe our world was created many millions of years ago as opposed to some who believe our world was created a few thousand years ago by some super human being who will not allow our world to be destroyed. There is a huge problem. Over population is destroying our world.

## EXPLOITATION AND OVER POPULATION

The resources in the world belong to every inhabitant in the world, including the animals of the world. And yet many resources have been depleted because of exploitation by a few inhabitants at the expense of everyone else.

For example one resource that has been depleted to a very dangerous level because of this exploitation is the forests of the world. Most of the  forests of the world have been totally eliminated and the rest of the forests are disappearing extremely fast.

The exploiters are the people living in the direct vicinity of the forests that destroy vast amounts of valuable forests for personal goals.

The exploiters are the lumber industry of the United States. No other country in the world has such capable exploiters of the world's forests as the US lumber industry.

There is a huge demand for lumber products and cleared land because of the masses of the human species that are populating the globe.

We  must work a lot harder at promoting birth control around the globe.

## ARE WE PLAYING WITH FIRE?

Have there been several other planets over the history of the universe that were very similar to our earth?

Is the reason why we never find other planets trying to communicate with us because the humans have always destroyed themselves leaving no one to communicate with?

Does it always signal the end of this type of planet when the human species over populates and over exploits?

The oxygen in the air we breathe has decreased by almost half in recent years.

Scientists have discovered that at one time the earth's air consisted of 38% oxygen. Today the air we breathe contains no more than 19 to 20% oxygen at the highest and in some areas as low as 11 to 13%. Oxygen breathing creatures cannot exist on less than 7% oxygen in the air. Is much of the oxygen on earth tied up in carbon dioxide? When oxygen disappears ozone also disappears. Ozone is oxygen.

When oxygen in the air diminishes another very important resource also starts to disappear, h2o, water.

More than 80% of the world's forests have been totally eliminated over the past 150 years. That is a shocking reduction in the oxygen generating plant life. But today probably more that 90% of the world's forests have already been totally destroyed. There have been no recent calculations of remaining forests. Massive destruction of forests has occurred in the past few years.

The remaining forests will disappear much faster now because there is much more demand for timber and tillable land due to over population by the human species.

Over the South Atlantic Ocean in the past several years there has been a continuous, huge blanket of smoke covering an area with a diameter up to 2000 miles across. This huge blanket of smoke is caused by the burning of rain forests in Africa and South America.

In Indonesia the smoke from burning rain forests is so thick it is a threat to life. It has been this way for several years. The smoke is spreading across much of Asia.

It is very possible that in the next few years things will start getting worse fast. The remaining forests are being destroyed faster today than ever before in the history of our world due to the demands of over population by the human species.

Of course if we don't do anything, we will probably find out in the next few years that this report has even more significance. But who knows when we have gone beyond the point of no return.

We must stop all forest tires around the world no matter what the cause. Time is running out. Soon there will be no forests left.

This should have been done yesterday. We must start working on it today like there was no tomorrow. Because if we don't there won't be.

The resources in the world belong to every inhabitant in the world, including the animals of the world. And yet many resources have been depleted because of exploitation by a few inhabitants at the expense of everyone else.

The holes in the ozone layer are caused by a shortage of oxygen. Ozone is oxygen. The ozone layer is our world's bubble of life. This ozone layer protects our planet from the hostile solar rays that cause all other planets of the universe to be hostile to living, oxygen breathing creatures. This is the same solar hostility that causes all other planets of the universe to be uninhabitable wasteland whipped by severe solar winds and scorched by solar rays. Extreme low temperatures and extreme high temperatures.

The nearly exclusive generator of oxygen on our planet is green plant life. Green plants use carbon dioxide like people use oxygen. They turn the carbon into fibers for their skeleton, structure and form. They release the oxygen into the air for ozone to protect us from the hostilities of the universe and oxygen for us to breathe.

The excess carbon dioxide in the atmosphere is the result of the extreme decrease in the green plant life of our world and, of course, excessive human population.

WE MUST DO SOMETHING!

We must bring back the green. We should go to the areas where the solar rays are coming through the hole in the ozone layer and test the effects they are having on the immediate environment. Do the solar rays penetrating the ozone layer and reaching the earth's surface overheat the oceans? Do the holes in the ozone layer cause the El Nino condition?

We should translate this report into the languages of the areas where the destruction of the forests is raging on out of control. We should distribute this report to the political powers of these regions. We should offer them help in fighting forest fires. We should educate the people who are destroying the rain forests of the vital role the rain forests play in the production of oxygen. We should encourage governments to restrict timber harvesting.

We must start tree planting activities. We should work through the free market. We cannot allow any political influence to interrupt or to slow the process.

Activities in the universe as compared to activities on our planet earth are extremely unfeeling and severely hostile to all forms of live. There is no compassion. There is no "second chance".

## SOCIALISM AND CAPITALISM

Socialism and Capitalism are combining to destroy the middle class. The middle class basically represents the free market. Crony Capitalism is basically a mixture of Socialism and Capitalism.

It seems all the power hungry groups are after the wealth of the wealth producer. The State Governments help the insurance industry and the litigation lawyers grab up the wealth of the wealth producer by passing laws such as compulsory insurance laws. The Democrats grab up the wealth of society in taxes. The Republicans encourage mergers and acquisitions and the result is more monopolies and less small businesses (small businesses produce more than 65% of all new jobs).

The management of corporations grab up the wealth of society through excessively high salaries for management and low wages for workers. The medical professions grab up the wealth in higher medical bills. The Federal Government creates monopolies with crony Capitalism. The Federal Government encourages monopolies and creates "too big to fail dinosaurs" by using tax payer money to bailing out corporations that should be allowed to fail. The wealth producer has to cover all of this. Welcome to the world of Capitalism.

There is more wealth produced with the Capitalists than with the Socialists because the wealth producer has more incentive to produce wealth in the Capitalist system.

It does not matter if it is a Democratic Government or a Dictatorship, if the laws take away an unfair share of the wealth produced by the workers of a society, as in taxes, that Government will not be popular.

In Socialism, (Dictatorships are usually socialist), because of inefficiency and because of lack of incentive to be productive, more wealth is consumed than is produced.

Free market is analytical type individual planning. Free market is ideas at work. Capitalism is money at work. Socialism is a central planning system.

The people of all societies want freedom to do their own planning and fairness, free from victimization, for the individual. But some members of society also want the easy life, or maximum leisure with minimum sweat or hard work or hardship. These two goals or demands of societies are conflicting goals. When the majority of a society demands the easy life and the minority demands individual freedom the Democratic Government of that society moves toward Socialism and away from free market.

But Socialism and central planning does not work because it eliminates incentives, challenges, opportunities and hardships which stimulate the brain to create ideas necessary for the existence of a free market and individual planning. It reduces analytical ability. The people of a Socialist society become tools to be used by the central planners to produce wealth for the central planners. They become slaves of the central planners. Without stimulating challenges, incentives and hardships the people become lazy mentally and physically and, therefore, nonproductive. They do not produce enough wealth to support the society.

The wealth of the society declines to the point where hardship overwhelms the society. The hardship causes the people of that society to wake up. The hardship stimulates and motivates the brain to start creating ideas as a means of survival. The society becomes analytical and aggressive. If a dictator doesn't lock the society into Socialism the society will decide that individual freedom and individual planning are necessary and that the society cannot exist in Socialism. Socialism is replaced by a Government that allows more individual freedom and planning. Indonesia is an example.

Eastern Europe is an example of the Socialist society. Fifty years of Socialism has brought the society of the Soviet Union to the hardship stage and to extinction.

The US Democracy has been mostly free market and individual planning but partly Socialist which seems to create something called capitalism. The people of the US society are demanding more of the easy life and, as a result, a more Socialist Government. As the constant addition of rules and regulations causes lifestyles to become easier, the hardships, challenges, risks and hazards disappear and the brain becomes less analytical because of this easy life.

Then the people tend to demand standards and guide lines because they cannot or do not want to determine right from wrong themselves. The result will be a loss of individual freedom and planning and more Socialism until the people have become tools for the central planners.

As the regulations on lifestyles, restrictions on individual planning and confiscation or transfer of wealth increases, the brain

143

power and wealth creators will leave the society. The remaining people in the society will become lazier and less wealth will be produced. The wealth of the society will decline and hardship will increase. If a strong, dictator type Government does not lock the society into Socialism, the society will demand that the Government change back to free market. This can take many years to develop. It took the Soviet Union fifty years. Japan has been doing it for over twenty years and counting.

In Western Europe the Governments are mostly Socialist and partly free market. In this type of Government the society seems to move sideways in time and the cycles from socialism to free market seem to be less abrupt or possibly nonexistent. This type of Government seems to move slowly toward more Socialism.

Hardship causes the people of a society to develop analytical ability. When the rules and laws are made to eliminate hardship the members of society do not have to use their brain power to solve the problems caused by hardship and the brain loses its analytical ability.

When socialism takes away the free market it eliminates the hardships that create the analytical ability and the self discipline the individual must have to solve his or her individual problems and to do the individual planning required in a free market.

When the majority of the population in a society has lost its analytical ability, the ability to solve its own problems, it then starts to demand that the Government furnish standards and guidelines. That is when the individuals of the society start to lose their freedoms in the best interest of the group or special interests or authoritarians. That is an invitation for Dictatorship, authoritarianism and Socialism. It is called "common good".

Socialism consists largely of organized groups of authoritarians, committees and special interests taking advantage of the individual wealth producer by robbing that individual of his or her wealth and freedom.

Socialism robs wealth producers through taxes and nationalization of industries and by eliminating property rights and with compulsory insurance.

Capitalism through monopolies robs wealth producers through unfair distribution such as excessively low wages at one end of the wage scale and excessively high salaries at the other end and unfair pricing and low quality products.

Capitalism robs wealth by lobbying for favorable legislation and contributing PAC money for politicians to restrict competition.

## FREE MARKET AND CAPITLISM

Free market is ideas at work. Capitalism is money at work. Free market is efficient because it disciplines itself. Free market is a market free of monopolies, price controls, subsidies, excessive taxation and regulations. Free market is a market free of restrictive Government regulations and other Government interference. Free market coordinates supply and demand. Free market rewards creative thinking and hard work. Competition in a free market encourages creative thinking and keeps the capitalists honest. Profit potential and incentive encourages creative thinking.

Free market is individual planning. Adam Smith's "invisible hand" remark about free market leaves a feeling of mystery about the free market idea. But the "invisible hand" is nothing more than individual planning. It is the opposite of "central planning".

Individual planning is the individual using his or her own analytical ability to solve his or her own problems, to determine right from wrong, to dream of future prosperity, to set goals and to determine priorities in his or her individual life, business or job as opposed to central planning where authoritarian figures do all the planning for the individual.

There are two ways to get a wealth producer to produce wealth. One way can encourage the wealth producer to produce his or her maximum and the other way will force the wealth producer to produce his or her minimum. One way is exciting and challenging wealth production, the other way is boring wealth production through forced labor, resentment, fear and threats. One way is the free market way through individual planning, incentives and Democracy. The other way is Socialism through central planning by dictators or authoritarian rule. One works, the other one not so well.

Nature is strongly competitive. In an ecological order in nature, dominant species and dominant specimens of a species rise to the top and force the weaker ones out. Stronger specimens constantly challenge weaker specimens and constantly keep the species in top condition.

Many of nature's functions are based on competition, survival of the species, survival of the fittest. The strongest and wisest competitor is the sire of the newborn. Nature and business both need competition.

Possibly in the free market society there is a similarity to the animals of the wild that roam freely. And a society controlled by central planning is similar to animals in a zoo.

In the wilderness where animals live by nature's rules the hazards and the elements of the wilderness make survival difficult. But these hazards and elements and difficulties will make society strong, wise and alert.

In free market new companies and ideas constantly challenge old companies and ideas and constantly keep the market in top competitive condition.

Governments that interfere with the free market through regulations, transfer of wealth schemes, compulsory mandates, restrictions and over taxation stop the flow of new ideas and the market loses its competitive strength. Monopolies develop, prices increase and quality decreases. Competition keeps prices of products fair and it increases quality of services and products. Anyone who does not believe in competition does not believe in free market.

These Government activities can also cause and usually do cause extreme fluctuation of prices and therefore unfair prices. These prices would not normally fluctuate unfairly in a free market system where the various Governments do not interfere.

However, if free market prices fluctuate wildly and the extreme price fluctuation is caused solely by the imbalance of supply or demand, such as the supply of food after a drought, and this fluctuation causes severe hardship, such as a threat to life and health of a society then the Governments should interfere with subsidies or regulations to relieve the imbalance. But only until the threat to life and health has disappeared. Then the Governments should dismantle the subsidies and regulations.

But the Governments should not interfere when true free market price fluctuation causes mild hardship that is not life or health threatening. The free market and the society need the mild pain and irritation of mild hardship to keep the free market and society mentally and physically alert, strong and healthy. The free market will naturally adjust to reduce the hardship and irritation.

All economies, given the opportunity to develop from the bottom up in a free market environment, are basically efficient wealth producing economies. Total free market challenges, incentives, pressures and restraints encourage basic economies to produce goods and services, demanded by consumers in the most efficient manner with the fairest prices and best quality.

It is impossible for any Government regulations to regulate any segment of the economy as efficiently, simply and fairly as real competition in a true free market.

There can be no such thing as over production in a true free market economy. When production exceeds demand, prices and profits will fall. Investment money will abandon low profit products and move to higher profit products.

When a new business is born it should be protected by the Federal Government from being harassed by unions and existing, thriving businesses, and local, and state Governments. An incubation period. But after the incubation period it should be forced to compete and to abide by all the rules of the competition.

Instead, today the Governments protect the existing, entrenched businesses and large corporations from new competition through regulations, licenses, insurance, restrictions, zoning laws and various taxes and monopolies.

This Government interference in the economy encourages and sometimes produces monopolies which result in higher prices, lower quality, fewer jobs and unfair distribution of wealth by restricting competition. This interference is also a large contributor to the homeless problem. It reduces jobs and prices necessities out of reach.

One of the most important freedoms of an individual is the freedom to choose his or her own source of income and then to have the freedom to collect and use the product of his or her sweat, the wealth.

**No one is entitled to a free ride. But when Government destroys opportunity, Government is responsible for the hardship.**

**If everyone is kind and nurturing but no one is producing wealth and everyone starts freezing and starving, where is the compassion in that?**

A competitive free market is a system where success is rewarded with wealth and failure is nothing more than a major educational tool that helps improve the individual wealth producer's chances of success.

In a society where the wealth producer is taxed excessively the ambitious and aggressive will leave the society because they have lofty goals and excessive taxation restricts their accomplishments. By driving high achievers out of the society the Government drives wealth out of the economy and thus reduces tax revenue.

If a society has a black market or underground economy then the Government is doing something wrong, usually over taxing or over

147

regulation or both. It is possible for the Government to reduce black markets or underground economies by authoritarian rule and severe consequences. But Government's authoritarian rule and severe disciplinary actions encourage flight of brain power and wealth and discourages production of wealth.

Black market is an example of people attempting to accept challenges, make plans and take risks in spite of suppressive Government activities. Aggressive people with fighting spirit are attempting to improve their personal life style or possibly, simply trying to earn a living in spite of restrictive laws. The capitalist system could be set up where the wealthy would benefit more by helping out the individual wealth producer than the wealthy would benefit by exploiting the individual wealth producer.

Free market was the main reason why the US was the number one economy in the world for 100 years. We need our free market back.

EMPLOYEE'S 29 HOUR WORK WEEK

The eight hour work day is too long. It creates an excessively rigid work force. This excessive rigidity is a large contributor to the unemployment problems in the Capitalist societies.

Also, a new wrinkle in the 40 hour week versus the less than 30 hour week comes from the Obama Care health bill. A 29 hour work week, considered a part time job, eliminates the health insurance requirement.

A less than six hour day, 29 hour week would be much more flexible. The workers of a society could be younger, and older because the shorter work day would be much easier than the eight hour work day. Young people could join the work force earlier and the older people could remain longer in the work force. The single parent could spend more time with the children. Plus, the 29 hour work week could possibly get around some other federal laws by claiming the employees as part time employees.

The person who wanted to speed up his or her accumulation of wealth could work a double shift of twelve hours much easier than a double shift of sixteen. Or he or she could work two different jobs with ease. The number of workers doing double shifts would have to be held below 50 employees in order to remain below the Obama Care requirements. In this "less than 50 employees group" could be a management crew.

When there were too many workers and too few jobs in a society the people working double shifts or two jobs could be reduced to a single shift or one job thereby opening up jobs for other workers. A flexible labor force.

When there were too many jobs and too few workers the capable workers could easily take on two shifts or two jobs. The need for unemployment insurance and pensions would be greatly reduced. The labor force would be much more flexible.

## IDIVIDUAL PLANNING, BUSINESS SYSTEM WITH INCENTIVE BONUSES

All businesses can use this individual planning system. It could increase productivity in small business dramatically. It's ability to compete would be so fierce that it would mean serious trouble for any business that used central planning.

With this special business idea of individual planning, the companies that use central planning will not have a chance. They will be run over by the fierce competition this idea can generate. It is not top down planning versus bottom up planning. It is central planning versus individual planning.

All employees could be hired at minimum wage hourly rate to start. This ongoing income would be paid similar to any other job. This income could be used to pay for groceries, transportation costs and surprise bills. But the real incentive that would draw ambitious, positive attitude employees would be that every quarter they would be paid a percentage of profits.

Example; Set any business up where all expenses are deducted from the gross income for the quarter including the minimum hourly wages. There could be any number of employees in the business but in this example there are 4 employees who's minimum wage income was deducted from the gross income.

After all expenses were deducted there was $30,000 leftover that I will call company profit for the quarter which will be split among all employees depending on their specific wage rates. The owner of the business will include himself as an average employee though it will not be necessary for him to be there managing the business. 'Selected' employees will run the business without him. With him included, that makes 5 employees.

2 employees make $4500 each in wages in the quarter.
2 employees make $5500 each in wages in the quarter.
The owner figures himself in at $5000.

2 @ $4500 = $9000
2 @ $5500 = $11000
1 @     $5000
Total wages   $25000

The total wages for the quarter was $25000 which was deducted as expenses. Each of the 2 employees at $4500 each would receive 4500/25000 or 18% of the $30,000 profits or $5400 for the quarter each. Each employee at $5500would receive 5500/25000 or 22% of the $30,000 of  profits or $6600 for the quarter each. The owner would receive 5000/25000 or 20% or  $6000 for the quarter.

This profit sharing plan would work  with any type of business. Add all employees' wages for the quarter together.  Then divide each employee's wages by the total  wages to find the percent of the profit each employee receives.

If the total wage rates were high then there would be less profit to split because the high wages would be deducted as expenses and would reduce the final profit.

If the total wage rates were lower, then there would be more profit to split.

If someone worked more hours in the quarter than the rest, His quarter's minimum wage income would be more accordingly and he would receive more of the profit at the end of the quarter.

All employees would have a say in  the operation of the business by voting. If one employee is not doing his or her fair share of the work a majority of the employees could vote to have him or her fired.  With their own profit sharing incomes on the line, existing employees would be very frugal in their decisions.

The wage rate per hour paid to each employee must be fair according to the skills of each employee.  All employees would start with the same base pay rate but for each skill an employee learned in addition to the base, he or she would receive a specific increase in pay rate.

Some employees would want to stay with one certain skill. Others would like to learn several skills.  They would be allowed to chose.  Their wage rates would be fairly adjusted accordingly.  The fairness would be determined by the majority of the employees.

There would be a trial period for each new employee and at the end of the trial period all employees that wanted to, would vote on whether the new employee would become a permanent employee. The majority would rule.

With a large group of employees a few would be elected by the workers as a committee to make operation decisions in which the owner could be involved.

The books must always be open for the employees to inspect.

If the owner was careful and selected honest, dependable employees to start with, the employees would maintain the quality of the employees and the owner could be an absent owner. The owner could set up several operations this way.

I want to emphasize how much difference there is in individual people and how important it is to select the most analytical, creative, honest, aggressive, ambitious individuals possible for the positions. You may find an individual with five years experience or with a formal education but the individual may be lazy or may not have analytical, creative ability or may not be dependable. A formal education or job experience is not as important as analytical ability, aggressiveness, positive attitude and dependability. The ideas of an aggressive, creative, analytical individual can be worth a fortune to a company. But to select a lazy, incompetent, undependable individual, no matter what the education, can be costly.

If the owner had loaned money to the company the payments would be deducted as expenses before the profit was divided. Also the owner could set up a cash flow fund where payments could be made before profit was divided. But if the owner became too greedy and reduced the profit too much the system could be a failure. The more profit to share the more incentive to produce, very important.

When companies change over to this individual planning, profit sharing idea, companies that use central planning will be left in the dust because the incentives in this individual planning idea will increase production dramatically and if the 29 hour work week mentioned above was integrated into the company, it would be a truly modern, competitive experience. The employees accumulated in this incentive system would be of highest quality and the main reason why it would be capable of huge success.

This is the ultimate business plan. This type of individual

business planning could compete against the biggest corporations that use central planning. This type of business plan is going to spread across the free market world and eliminate all central planning. The success of this incentive plan would depend on the fairness and size of the incentive.

Many large corporations will have no choice but to break up and down size. Competition will be too great.

Turn small business lose. It can produce much more wealth than large corporations can.

INSURANCE

If the Government is going to bail out private enterprise with tax payer money why do we even have an insurance industry?

Insurance is similar to but opposite of gambling. You are paying in advance for problems you think you might have in the future. The question is, do the costs of the problems ever add up to the costs of the premiums. For the cautious person, the costs of the premiums usually add up to way more than the costs of the problems. That is one reason why insurance should never be mandated. But that is the main reason why insurance is mandated, so the cautious can carry the careless, so the cautious can be enslaved to the careless and the insurance industry.

As the cautious and intelligent, wise up to the discrepancy and stop buying insurance, the industry is put into a bind. So the Government bails out the insurance industry with mandates. The excess paid in premiums go to the middle man insurance industry. The insurance industry calls itself a pass through mechanism. In other words a transfer of wealth mechanism.

The insurance industry pays for the various problems that it insures, but the payment procedure is so hidden from view of the consumer, so short on transparency that the costs of solving the various problems skyrocket completely out of control. Plus the consumer that has paid for the protection does not care how much the insurance industry pays the maintenance industry as long as he or she does not have to pay. Who knows what kind of deal the insurance industry has with the maintenance industry.

There is one industry, the insurance industry, that appears to be a parasite industry. I can't think of any way that it helps wealth producers to produce more wealth. The insurance is a trillion dollar a year industry.

Does insurance really, actually reduce risk? Is it really, anything more than a group of middle men and women being carried by the wealth producer? (Even if it did reduce risk, the risk is much more valuable than the insurance because risk is a very important educational tool.) When you insure risk, you are paying a middle man and that always increases the cost of risk. But it also separates the provider from the customer and that separation and obscurity always allows costs to go out of control. When insurance is involved no one knows what the price is or should be. It is one of the main reasons why health care is so expensive.

"Who cares if the bill is inflated by 500%, 1000% as long as I don't have to pay it". That is the attitude of everyone when insurance takes over the risks and payments to the maintenance industry. Somebody has to pay it. Do you suppose it could massively increase the price of premiums and profits for the insurance and maintenance and insurance industries?

The transfer of wealth industry. Even the insurance industry calls insurance a pass through mechanism. A trillion dollar a year pass through mechanism.

If it does not help the wealth producer produce more wealth then it is a trillion dollar a year waste of wealth because the wealth producer is carrying it. If it does not produce wealth it is a drag on the economy. It is a parasite.

Universal, mandated or compulsory insurance of any kind required by Governments is punishment to the prudent, the competent, the successful, the healthy people of a society. The competent are forced to carry the incompetent. The responsible are forced to carry the reckless and irresponsible. The hard workers are forced to carry the lazy. The healthy are forced to carry the unhealthy. I would say that is getting pretty close to slavery for the workers.

It is worse than taxation because the cost increases without notice and without restriction. It is an incentive for the competent, successful, prudent, responsible, hard working wealth producers of a society to be lazy, incompetent, irresponsible and reckless. Compulsory insurance is a form of SOCIALISM! Compulsory insurance is also a subsidy for the insurance industry at the expense of the consumer.

Of course the health insurance industry will bend over backward to get a health plan that requires everyone to buy health insurance. They know a windfall when they see it. Compulsory health insurance is not fair to members of our society who seriously maintain a healthy lifestyle.

Fairness would be improved greatly if the Government produced incentives that encouraged people to develop healthy lifestyles as opposed to forcing the healthy to carry the unhealthy with compulsory insurance.

Health insurance causes the health industry to be excessively opaque. There is not enough truth, not enough reality. No one knows what the price is or should be. When an industry is so opaque or its real activities so invisible, when no one knows what is going on, all the greedy participants go crazy with obscene charges in order to collect as much as possible. Similar to a monopoly.

Insurance should be totally eliminated from the health industry. The parasite middle men and women should be banned from the health industry. Forcing the middle man out and causing the patient and medical personnel to deal directly with each other is the only way to make the health industry transparent and efficient. The only way to increase truth and reality and bring down costs.

If the insurance middle man was eliminated and the patient was allowed to deal directly with the health provider, health care in the United States would not be nearly as expensive. In fact, I am convinced that if the health insurance industry was eliminated, the US society would be absolutely amazed to find out how much the industry is costing society. Health costs would become surprisingly affordable.

If the true, realistic goal of the medical industry is to make humans healthier then the demand and need for medical care should be declining. The society should be getting healthier and the medical industry should be shrinking not growing. Obviously the medical industry has a different goal.

Do you know why animals of the wild do not need a trillion dollar a year medical system? Because they go by natures rules. Who said that people are smarter than animals?

Of all the health care plans promoted by politicians, the individual medical savings accounts are by far the best because they bring the providers and patients together by eliminating the middle men and women, they have the INCENTIVE and potential to save money, they are transferable from job to job and they do not discriminate against people with preconditions.

The reasons why individual medical savings accounts are not

popular is because they do not give the politicians enough control over health issues and because the health industry cannot make enough obscene profits For these reasons many Democrats and Republicans are against them.

If the States did not make 'blame the other guy' type auto insurance mandatory, auto repair would not be nearly as expensive. 'No fault' auto insurance would be beneficial to the economy because the people would have a choice whether to have insurance or not and the competent consumer would not have to carry the incompetent and the insurance industry and the auto body industry. If a person decided to have insurance, the policy would cover all of that person's loses. It would not matter who was at fault.

Eliminate all insurance mandates. Insurance mandates make slaves out of the competent, healthy, careful, responsible wealth producers. Insurance is an attempt to eliminate risk. Insurance is an attempt to compensate for mistakes. Insurance employees are middle men. It is a transfer of wealth from the wealth producer to the insurance industry. The insurance industry does not produce any wealth. IT IS A TRILLION DOLLAR A YEAR PARASITE!

## SHOULD THE GOVERNMENT NATIONALIZE THE INSURANCE INDUSTRY?

Since transparency is almost nonexistent in the insurance industry, their ability to increase profit margins is out of control. I believe the main reason to nationalize the insurance industry would be to eliminate the profit incentive. The profit incentive is a big incentive for a parasite industry to be even more expensive and destructive. Health insurance is an example. Auto insurance is another example. But rather than nationalize it, the best move would be to outlaw insurance.

INSURANCE, the transfer of wealth industry.

Trillion dollar a year pass through mechanism. That is what the insurance industry calls itself, a pass through mechanism. In other words it is a middle man in the transfer of wealth and it is very secretive about how it transfers that wealth. The Government should discourage wealth transfer. Instead, it is the biggest instigator of wealth transfer.

The insurance industry thrives on accidents. If there were no accidents there would be no risk. There would be no need for insurance. The more accidents happen in a society the more society feels a need for protection from that risk, the ideal situation for the insurance industry. I am not saying the insurance industry encourages accidents but they don't try very hard to discourage them either.

Since the insurance industry does not produce wealth, it must depend on the transfer of wealth for its income. And since it does not produce its own wealth it must constantly convince low risk people to buy its insurance policies. As the bureaucracy of the insurance industry grows and the prices of premiums rise the premiums obviously become less valuable. The low risk people can see they are better off taking the risk and resist buying the premiums. Now the high risk people are the only ones that can see any value in buying insurance.

The insurance industry lobbied for compulsory insurance because they wanted the low risk citizen who does not tend to be a big insurance customer to be forced to buy insurance and thereby subsidize the high risk individual who tends to be an active insurance customer but more costly than the low risk person.

Plus, they raised prices because they wanted better profits. The low risk individual did not buy insurance because the cost of the insurance was higher than the benefit. As the insurance industry raised prices, more people decided not to buy insurance. Intelligent, cautious responsible people were not buying insurance because of the exploding costs. The insurance industry was going broke. With mandatory insurance they were free to raise prices and profits. They had a captive customer.

The insurance industry makes its money by spreading and transferring risk into the future and from the high risk individual to the low risk individual. If they keep their activities as secret as possible, they can adjust the prices to their benefit.

When you had an accident and the insurance company raised the cost of your premium then you were paying for the past accident plus your future accidents plus their profits (and possibly other people's accidents). That was ok before compulsory insurance laws, people still had a choice of whether or not to buy insurance. But then the insurance industry got greedy and lobbied for compulsory insurance laws.

These laws passed the risk and the cost of accidents from the high risk to the low risk, from the deserving to the undeserving. This was not fair. This was selecting winners and losers. This unfairness builds resentment and hostility toward Government. Compulsory insurance laws may be an example of the individual becoming a slave to the special interests.

There are different types of risk. There is the risk a person takes when he invests in a business as opposed to investing in a relatively risk free money market fund. He is going to have some hardships and failures. But these hardships and failures are going to educate him. He is going to become an intelligent, tough, competitive business man. He will have the potential and the intelligence to increase his wealth much more rapidly than the individual who chose to take no risk.

Another type of risk is the risk of tragedy or catastrophe resulting from natural causes such as storms and earth quakes, forest fires and range fires that get out of control. This type of risk can be life threatening. The damages and losses can be shocking. The Government does and should get involved in this type of disaster.

Another type of risk is the risk of accidents caused by negligence. If there was no compulsory insurance law and an individual chose to drive without insurance, as opposed to buying insurance coverage, the obvious risk that individual accepted would cause his or her to develop cautious, courteous, defensive driving skills that would give that person the potential to avoid serious accidents. That individual would have the potential and the ability to drive all his or her life without being involved in a serious accident. Look at the thousands of dollars that person would save in insurance premiums. Look at all the accidents that type of driving skill would prevent.

If a person pays twenty five hundred dollars a year for auto insurance and the person never has an accident in his or her life, consider this. In ten years that is twenty five thousand dollars. Twenty years it is fifty thousand. Forty years that is a hundred thousand dollars spent on insurance that the person did not need. In a mandatory insurance environment, that one hundred thousand dollars went to pay for someone else's carelessness and someone else's profits. That is absolutely unfair. If the individual who was careless and received the one hundred thousand dollars of protection, instead, had to pay the one hundred thousand dollars it would be a tremendous incentive to be more careful.

Accidents do not just happen. Accidents are caused by carelessness, thoughtlessness, poor judgment and lack of consideration. If there was no insurance available and the individual who was careless and thoughtless and used poor judgment had to face the risks involved in an accident caused by that person's carelessness he or she would improve his or her habits. That would be beneficial to everyone.

But if that same individual chose to buy insurance coverage and reduce his or her risk, he or she would develop a false sense of security and would be less cautious, taking more chances and developing bad habits such as running red lights, following too close, not watching where he or she is going and driving too fast. Insurance coverage reduces risk and thereby reduces alertness and encourages bad habits and reckless driving that in turn causes accidents.

In this train of thought risk is an educational tool. Risk causes people to develop cautious, courteous and defensive driving skills. When this valuable educational tool is eliminated drivers become less alert, more careless and reckless and thereby cause more accidents. Compulsory insurance laws contribute to the increase in accidents.

Also, if there was no insurance industry raising the costs of repair and insurance premiums, the cost of repairs would be much lower.

Accidents do not have near the same meaning to a person who does not have to pay for an accident, who merely turns it over to an insurance agency. The intended educational purposes of accidents are totally lost and the individual will be more careless and have more accidents because of it.

If a person does not have auto insurance and has an accident the cost of accidents would effectively tend to prohibit the accident prone individual from driving or would force him or her to learn to drive cautiously and defensively due to direct economic pressures.

Having insurance does not reduce the risk of having an accident. In fact having insurance increases the risk of having an accident. A person who has insurance develops a false sense of security. The individual with insurance becomes much more careless than the individual who does not have insurance. There is a bumper sticker that reads, "HIT ME, I NEED THE MONEY". If that individual did not have insurance do think he or she would be displaying that bumper sticker? Definitely not. In fact the bumper sticker implies that the individual needs the money bad enough that he or she will "HELP YOU HIT" him or her. Everyone has heard about the people who cause accidents on purpose with the intention of collecting insurance benefits.

Imagine a modern US society where insurance was absolutely unheard of. There would be no more hostile people shaking accusing fingers at their neighbors screaming, "It's your fault! I'm going to sue!". Hostility toward our neighbors would be greatly reduced. Insurance seems to bring out the malice and hostility in the best of us. We find ourselves threatening to sue our own friends and relatives.

Insurance companies tend to develop a Gestapo type authoritarian attitude which can cause stress and anxiety that can be hazardous to a person's health. If you are involved in an accident the other person's insurance company will send you a threatening letter, whether you have insurance or not, threatening that if you do not have insurance, you are doomed. They list the steps they are going to take that will blast you into permanent slavery. If you cannot find your "proof of insurance slip" to show the attending officer, the Department of Motor Vehicles will send you a threatening notice of possibility of surprisingly high fines, loss of license and imprisonment. Through state mandates, the consumer is threatened by loss of wealth through extremely high fines and loss of license and imprisonment. In other words, total loss of the use of his or her car which is essential for his or her livelihood, loss of wealth and possible loss of his or her job. This can be an extreme hardship on a low income family.

Governments force the consumer to buy insurance through these threats. This is the type of situation the insurance industry and the litigation lawyers had hoped and lobbied for. Now the insurance industry and the litigation lawyers have a Government established monopoly. They can raise the rates and lower the coverage and use the laws to threaten the citizens.

The insurance industry is another industry the Socialists love to take over along with the oil and gas industry. They can legislate mandates and collect the forced revenue. It is even a better revenue source that collecting taxes.

Neither a Government nor a society should encourage an insurance industry. In fact a society and economy would be much better off if the insurance industry was discouraged. People of the insurance industry are merely middle men and women who transfer wealth and risk from the deserving to the undeserving. The insurance industry contributes very little, if anything to the production of wealth or safety in a society. No other economy in the world is so unbalanced by an insurance industry as the US is.

If there is an insurance policy that actually helps a business or individual produce more wealth, then that insurance policy is a wealth producing insurance policy. But if the business or individual could

159

produce more wealth or retain more of the wealth produced without the insurance policy, then the money paid for the insurance policy is a transfer of wealth.

In the US the mandatory transfer of wealth caused by federal, state and local compulsory insurance laws has helped the parasite insurance industry grow to many times the size it should be. Billions of dollars of wealth are transferred annually from the deserving to the undeserving. The insurance industry is the major cause of the extreme high rate of cost increases in the health care and health insurance industries and the auto insurance and auto repair industries in the US.

I was involved in a little incident at a service station where a vehicle I owned broke the handle on a nozzle at the end of the hose and put a small dent in the cover panel on the side of the pump. Nothing else was damaged. I estimated that 300 dollars would have been an exceptionally high bill for damages done. I told my insurance agent and the service station owner I would like to pay for damages in order to keep my insurance record clear. I asked the service station owner what the damage would be. He said about 3000 dollars. I told my insurance agent about the ridiculous charge. He said, "there is nothing I can do about it". This type of insurance activity goes on every day. That same insurance agent told me that he spent $13,000 every year on Christmas decorations.

I know If there was no insurance company involved I would not have paid more than 300 dollars for damages. That is one example of how ridiculous the charges by insurance companies increase when there is no restricting force guarding against excessive charges. If all charges to insurance companies are multiplied by ten or more when there is no restrictive force controlling charges I can see how the insurance industry does a trillion dollars worth of business per year. And that amount is rising fast.

A wealth producer has respect for the wealth he or she produces because he or she sweat for that wealth and will spend it carefully and efficiently. A person or Government that receives transferred wealth has no respect for that wealth and will use it wastefully and irresponsibly.

Not only insurance people, but professionals such as doctors and lawyers use insurance payments in various ways to ratchet up their own incomes and in some instances as a total source of income. Insurance payments are bonuses to the professions because on top of the insurance payments they will also collect as much of the hospital patient's and the accident victim's money as they possibly can.

Agreed, the expenses of hospitalization and auto repair is extremely high and difficult for most individuals to cover. But if the auto repair industry and medical services industry did not have access to the lucrative and easy insurance revenue to pad their income these expenses could and would be reduce considerably. If the person receiving the service dealt directly with the service provider and if the wealth producer was paying his or her own bill this would be a restrictive force guarding against excessive charges.

What purpose compulsory insurance? Is it to help the insurance industry make more money? It sure does that. It also helps various professions make more money. Do the politicians who vote for this type of legislation collect some form of kick back?

When a state passes compulsory insurance laws and that state does not have an insurance industry with company headquarters in that state, then all the money the citizens of that state spend on insurance flows out of the state with the exception of course of the percent the insurance agents retain. The rest of the money goes to the state where the headquarters of the insurance is located. In other words there is a tremendous outflow of wealth from the state that requires insurance but does not have an insurance industry. Any politician who votes for such compulsory insurance and allows the wealth to flow out of the state is a hazard to the economy of the state.

The Government should require that all insurance be "no fault" insurance. The Government should require that in this "no fault" insurance the insurance company of the insured party would have absolutely no interest in who was at fault in an accident.

The insurance company would pay only the losses of its own policy holders. The victim of an accident who had paid for insurance coverage would have all his expenses taken care of by his insurance company, including injury and property loss expenses. The insurance company or the victim would have absolutely no interest in the other insurance companies involved in the accident or their policy holders or anyone involved who did not have insurance. The insurance company would not try to determine who was at fault. There would be no hostile jockeying for position for a possible court battle or a financial settlement.

The person or company involved in the accident who did not have insurance would pay for his or her or their own losses. In an accident where there was a victim or someone was at fault or someone broke the law, the law enforcement and the courts would handle all these situations and restrict litigation. No insurance company would or should be involved. Of course if the auto was purchased with a loan the loan company would still require insurance to protect its interests.

In a society where the insurance is true no fault and where there are no compulsory insurance laws requiring insurance coverage, there will be no litigation as we know it today. There will be no search for deep pockets. The insurance company will pay only the losses of the individual who pays the premiums. It will eliminate hundreds of millions of dollars spent each year to pay for litigation and excessive settlements and excessive profits.

Litigation is caused by Government. The Government is allowing the wealth producer to be victimized by litigation lawyers. Litigation is usually a case of extreme over reaction in which the intended goal is to transfer huge amounts of wealth. Those hundreds of millions of dollars are collected by ever increasing insurance premiums paid by individuals and businesses. This is simply a transfer of wealth. There is no wealth produced to make the society richer. In other words the litigation lawyers and insurance companies are parasites confiscating the wealth produced by the individuals and businesses, the wealth producers of our society. All branches of Government should restrict litigation because it effectively robs the wealth producer more than any other member of society.

If the Government would do its job and protect the wealth producer from being victimized by litigation, a prudent, efficient, careful, intelligent, health conscious individual would not need insurance of any kind.

The part of the insurance business that tries to protect the individual from his or her own mistakes or the mistakes of others is a dangerous activity that tends to weaken society. Mistakes are nature's own educational tool. Every member in a society that is successful is successful because of his ability to solve problems created by mistakes and hazards and difficulties.

Mistakes are more educational than successes. Without mistakes there would be no successes. When the effects of mistakes are eliminated or weakened any educational value is also weakened by the same proportion. A Chinese proverb says "Pain makes man think, thought makes man wise". It stands to reason if you eliminate the pain, the man won't be quite so wise.

The attempt to eliminate pain and suffering or to limit it is basically a distortion. It just transfers the pain from one place to another or doubles the pain. When a person is compensated for pain and suffering the bill is inevitably passed on to the innocent consumer or wealth producer. And when the pain is transferred to the innocent wealth producer it is a different type of pain and the educational experience is also different. The wealth producer is discouraged and becomes a little less productive.

Pain and suffering is nature's educational tool. Suppose a person is struck by lightning. That person's family will suffer pain, will suffer trauma, emotional stress. But what is the family going to do? They can't sue God.

Nature never intended for anyone to be compensated for pain and suffering. Accidents, mistakes all cause pain and suffering. For every mistake you make you will suffer is some way. The suffering is intended to educate. If you suffer you will decide it is not worthwhile to make the mistake again and the mistake will be eliminated. It is educational. The more mistakes an individual makes, the more the individual appreciates success when it finally arrives. If mistakes are not made then the success will not even be recognized as success.

Another reason why it is unfair for a few to receive payment for pain and suffering and for the majority not to receive payment is that the wealth producer ultimately has to pay for that payment that the few receive. No matter which "deep pockets" appears to be paying for the huge settlement, the bill always gets passed back to the wealth producer through higher prices. It is a transfer of wealth.

What is the purpose of compulsory auto insurance? Is it in the best interest of the public? Hardly! What the State is saying is, "You do business with this specific industry or lose your privilege to drive". It is not a privilege any more. It is a necessity. It is more of a necessity than insurance will ever be. That is an example of the loss of a freedom and necessity for the benefit of a special interest.

State legislation that makes auto insurance compulsory is supporting and establishing a monopoly for the insurance industry. Compulsory insurance laws are forcing the wealth producer to become a slave of the insurance industry.

The State compulsory auto insurance law is worse than a tax because it is impossible to keep the insurance industry from raising the cost of insurance which the industry will definitely do when it has a hostage customer.

For young couples who do not have enough experience in the work force and cannot demand much more than minimum wage, the State compulsory insurance laws are an extreme burden. Especially considering the insurance rates for young people are much higher than for older people. And especially since most of them are too young to vote and have no way of demanding fairness from the elected officials.

The cost of owning a car or truck could be reduced by a significant amount if insurance was not required. In many instances today the annual insurance premium costs more than the vehicle is worth. This excessive, unnecessary expense contributes, in a big way, to the homeless problem. In the case of poor families the cost of insurance can put personal transportation beyond their reach. Even if it does not, it still adds an unnecessary load. Without personal transportation many jobs are also out of reach.

Compulsory insurance is an attempt to force the frugal, efficient, aggressive and productive citizen to pay for the health problems and the accidents of the incompetent, careless, lazy and inefficient citizen. What it does is breed incompetence, inefficiency, resentment and laziness. Because if a person who is frugal, who spends time and takes care to improve his efficiency and to improve his production has to carry the inefficient, lazy, incompetent individual he is discouraged, he is irritated when it is forced upon him. It is an incentive for him to also be lazy, incompetent and unproductive. And the incompetent and indifferent individual will become even more incompetent and indifferent because the educational tool of "risk" has been removed.

The sickly have already spent their money on medical expenses so where are they going to get more money? From the healthy people. Laws that make insurance compulsory. Then the healthy will have to give up their money to pay for the medical expenses of the sickly.

An individual who is careful and avoids accidents or maintains good health through exercise and healthful eating habits can save a large amount of his or her accumulated wealth by not buying insurance or by not being involved in accidents or by not getting sick and paying medical bills. Why should this individual be discriminated against or victimized by laws that require him or her to give up significant amounts of his or her wealth to carry individuals who carelessly destroy their own health through poor diet and laziness or who have careless and reckless

164

habits?

Nearly all business insurance premiums are passed on to the consumer. Businesses include all expenses of doing business, including a certain percent of profit in the price of the products those businesses sell. In other words the consumer pays for all of business's expenses and profits. If businesses did not do this they would go broke.

When a farmer sells an apple to a wholesaler, he includes a portion of his insurance costs in the price of that apple. The trucker who transports that apple includes a part of his insurance costs in the rate he charges for transporting that apple. The wholesaler includes a portion of his costs of insurance along with a portion of his other expenses including the price he paid the farmer and the transportation expenses in the price he charges the retailer for that apple.

The retailer includes the price he paid the wholesaler and a portion of his insurance expenses along with his other expenses and a percentage of profit in the price he charges for the apple.

When all of those concerns have finished doing business and tally up their income they have passed all of their insurance costs to the consumer. A significant amount of the price of that apple is used to pay for the insurance costs of all those business concerns.

It is not just the price of the apple that absorbs all of the expenses of doing business. Apply the same routine to the prices of everything the consumer buys. It seems as if there is a hidden pipe line where the consumer's wealth flows to the insurance industry through the prices of products and services not to mention the premiums the consumer pays directly.

This is a huge transfer of wealth from you and me to the insurance industry. A trillion dollar a year industry that does not create any wealth. In other words, a trillion a year parasite that is carried by the wealth producer. But that is not nearly as bad as the Federal Government, a 16 trillion dollar a year parasite carried by the wealth producer. Pretty soon we are going to be talking "Big Money".

This insurance cost also increases the price of US exports significantly enough to make them less competitive in foreign markets. All products sold, whether in the US or exported have to have the cost of insurance included in their price. We wonder why our products are not competitive on the world market, why we have a trade deficit. No other country in the world has as high an insurance bill as the US wealth producer. The US insurance industry does business to the tune of one trillion dollars annually. That is a huge percent of the gross national product.

Liability insurance is the absolute reverse of what nature intended. Nature intended that when a person made a mistake he or she should pay for that mistake in some form of hardship. This way the individual learns from the mistake and tends not to make the mistake again. But insurance takes the cost, the hardship away from the person who made the mistake and passes it on to innocent people who pick up the bill for the insured person's mistake. The person who makes the mistake suffers no hardship. Since he does not have to pay, he does not mind making the mistake again. The penalty payments for his mistake are passed on to the innocent individual through higher insurance premiums.

Hardship and risk is as old as life itself. Hardship and risk are both necessary to strengthen the character of the individual and as a result strengthen the society. We must not allow anyone, including Government, to totally eliminate hardship or risk. Eliminating hardship or risk will reduce the strength of character of the individual and as a result will reduce the strength of a society. Hardship and risk are part of Nature's regulatory system.

Insurance takes away an individual's responsibility to solve his own problems. The individual loses character as he loses responsibility. This also reduces an individual's ability to make responsible decisions. He then loses his determination and ability to solve his own problems. This weakens society.

Insurance people are middle men who prey upon the threat of some future disaster to scare people into buying insurance. If the truth was known, the majority of us who buy insurance pay far more in insurance premiums in our life time than we ever collect in settlements. In other words the risks are not nearly as bad as we are led to believe. The litigation lawyer is a parasite preying upon a parasite, the insurance industry. The wealth producers, the consumers, the individuals and the businesses who buy the premiums pay for every bit of it.

Members of the insurance industry are professional middle men in the transfer of wealth. These professional middle men are taking advantage of the individual who has had an accident. They drum up hysteria and flaunt risk in order to make their position as middle man in the transfer of funds from the victim of an accident to the repair man and the medical profession look valid. But for this service of middle man they collect a substantial fee.

The victim of an accident has to pay not only the repair man and the medical profession but also the fee of the middle man. And since the victim is not paying his or her own bills to the repairman and the medical profession there is no restriction on the costs and, as a result, costs skyrocket. They also pay for the fees of litigation lawyers and all the ridiculously high awards and settlements the litigation lawyers cause to come about. They also pay bonuses to the professions through the insurance payments to the professions.

This middle man does not reduce the risk of having an accident nor does he eliminate or reduce the cost of having an accident. In fact he increases the cost of living in our society to be much higher than it would be if he was not present.

No Government should be allowed to force an individual to do business with any industry. The individual should be allowed the freedom to determine where his wealth should be spent. It should be unconstitutional for any Government, Federal, State or Local to require compulsory insurance.

The Federal Government should protect the individual from State laws requiring insurance of any kind. Compulsory laws that force an individual to do business with any industry may be considered a form of slavery. For a State to require an individual to buy any product from an industry is worse than any tax law because when the industry has a monopoly established by a Government the industry finds a way to raise prices dramatically. The individual is unfairly forced to transfer a continuously and dramatically increasing amount of his wealth to the industry.

The cost of insurance will continue to go up as people find new ways to take advantage of the deep pockets.

Litigation and lawsuits transfer wealth from the wealth producer to the undeserving. Insurance premiums do the same. The insurance industry has become another form of justice system in the US, punishing people for making the slightest mistake and many times for making no mistake at all as in the search for deep pockets.
See - IS HEALTH CARE A BASIC RIGHT? Page 39

MONEY
In a recession consumer spending and business spending or consumption falls because they have lost their source of income or have

become cautious.    The consumers and businesses are retaining income or looking for a job or a real tax cut or looking for less Government interference in the economy.   But if the Governments enact short term tax cuts (tax cuts must be long term) or tax increases or increase regulations or reduces the value of the currency, confidence will not improve.

The economy would benefit much more if the taxes were not increased and the interest rate remained high thereby keeping the value of the currency higher and if the Government would stay out of the way. When the value of the currency goes down, the standard of living goes down with it.  When the value of the currency remains high the standard of living remains high.  Consumers love a strong currency.

In order for the consumer to start buying again he or she must realize an increase in income and reduced Government interference. When the Governments enact long term tax cuts and reduce regulations the consumer will develop confidence in the economy.

When there is a recession the local Governments should reduce restrictions and requirements for new businesses to the point than it is easier to start a business than it is to get a job.

When the economy went into recession in the early  eighties it was not caused by the Federal Reserve reducing the money supply, it was the fact that Congress decided to wait until 1982 to put the tax cuts into effect.  If they had made the tax cuts effective immediately there would not have been a recession.

When Carter increased the money supply in the late 1970's, the money was not used to expand or create new jobs.  The big corporations used the money to buy up existing businesses after the economy turned around in the 1980's.   This was the beginning of the merger and acquisition craze that reduced the number of small businesses and created monopolies.

## MONOPOLIES VERSUS COMPETITION

We cannot question the fact that the Toyota and Volkswagen competition in the past for the US auto industry was very beneficial to the US economy.  In fact over the years this foreign competition was very beneficial in that it helped keep US auto prices down and quality up.

Why didn't the  US business community respond and give the big auto industry this competition right here in our own country?  The

Government, even then, was passing regulations that protected the big auto manufacturers from competition. In fact, there were several companies that tried and went broke; Studebaker, Hudson, Kaiser-Frazer, American Motors. The Government should have helped them compete rather than restricting them.

This is just one example but the examples of companies and industries that have built themselves up into monopolies, thanks to Government protection, can be found throughout the US economy.

Even a group of five or six big companies that control an industry can become a form of monopoly through crony capitalism and price fixing. The defense industry is an example, the medical industry is an example - industrial monopolies

If the US, City, County and State Governments as well as the Federal Government had not passed so many restrictive regulations the US businesses would and could compete with any foreign competition and the middle class would still exist. The restrictions and zoning have been put into place to protect the existing businesses , the special interests. This protectionism eliminates competition. It limit's the entrepreneurial activity. It prices US products out of foreign markets. It weakens the creative ability and competitive ability of US business.

This is all thanks to the Government because the Government did not encourage competition. In fact the Government restricted competition. In fact there was a lot of regulations and crony capitalism with Government helping big corporations develop monopolies.

In the oil industry in the early 1990's the big oil companies developed monopolies in the gasoline market by trading their stations in distant areas for the competing company's stations in their area. One company trades stations far away from its refineries and headquarters for stations close to its refineries and headquarters. In that way they eliminate competition and develop monopolies. Without the competition they can control prices.

No business has a right to a monopoly. No Government should be allowed to create monopolies or allow monopolies to exist. No Government should choose winners and losers.

Monopolies can collect an extremely unfair amount of the society's wealth through higher prices and lower quality. That is why today's corporate executives are way overpaid. No competition to keep them efficient.

The individual has a right to a fair share of the wealth he or she produces. The individual consumer has a right to the lowest prices and highest quality and largest variety of products that competition in a free market can produce. If the Government would help small businesses compete against monopolies, the economy would expand dramatically. Small businesses create many more jobs than big companies and corporations.

In a free market, profit is the main goal. It will be natural for profit seeking corporations to attempt price fixing or price gouging and try to create monopolies in order to realize maximum profit. Profit seekers will also attempt to market low quality products and services in order to maximize profits. Managers of these corporations will increase their salaries as much as possible. Competition will force these profit seekers to fall in line or go out of business.

There cannot be too much competition. If there is too much competition, some competitors will drop out. Competition is one of the best regulations the economy could ever have. Free market is efficient because it disciplines itself with competition. Free market is a market free of monopolies, price controls excessive regulation and subsidies. Free market coordinates supply and demand. Free market rewards creative individual thinking and hard work. Competition in a free market encourages creative thinking. Oh, what fun!

It is natural for capitalism to creating monopolies. It is natural for capitalism to attempt to make as much profit as possible. It is up to the Government to see that the individual is not over charged, that there are no victims. It is up to the Government to restrict monopolies and encourage competition. It is up to the Government to control the exuberance.

In a recession or depression the various Governments should cut taxes and reduce the regulations and restrictions to the point that it would be easier to start up a business than it would be to get a job. This would be much simpler, faster, more successful, more direct and more efficient than using the method Keynes suggested, having Government increase spending.

Keynes worried too much about savings and investment. Attention should be aimed at demand. If the consumer can afford the things he demands, investment will find a way to satisfy the demand. A consumer must have wealth or there will be no economy. When Governments take away the consumer's wealth through taxes and businesses do not allow consumers to retain wealth by keeping wages too low, the economy is reduced accordingly. They cannot satisfy their demand and no amount of investment will cure that. Investment cannot be forced upon any economy. Investment must be led by demand.

But if the consumer has wealth, consumption will follow naturally. Consumption happens when consumers satisfy demand. The more wealth the consumer has the more consumption there will be. As the consumer accumulates more wealth, more small businesses will start up to satisfy the new demand. This is opportunity for the welfare recipient, the poor and the homeless to get a job and also start up a business of his or her own, potentially eliminating welfare and the homeless problem.

Consumers need opportunities to accumulate wealth such as jobs and business opportunities. Consumers are the economy. Government must be careful what type of regulations they legislate.

Sometimes competitive free markets can impose hardships on the wealth producers. But Governments should not be too quick to offer subsidies and pass laws to regulate and thereby reduce hardships. Hardships, as long as they are not so severe that they threaten lives, will significantly strengthen a wealth producer's endurance and creative ability.

A competitive free market is a system where success is rewarded with wealth and failure is nothing more than a major educational tool that helps improve the individual wealth producer's chances of success.

Hardship causes development of creative minds, ideas, entrepreneurs. The entrepreneurs create new jobs and new products. They create new jobs and give existing businesses competition which helps reduce prices and helps increase quality.

This same theory of hardship can be applied to corporations. This will help to make the corporation a creative competitor. Governments should not be too quick to rush in with protectionism. Protection through Government regulation subsidies, trade embargos and tariffs can cause businesses to become lazy, inefficient, uncreative and uncompetitive, weakening the economy.

I know a worker does not like others competing for his or her job. It means he or she must work harder and the individual cannot demand as much in wages. But a society needs competition even in the labor sector. If the workers do not have competition, production will decrease, quality will decrease, workers will become lazy. The society will be a weaker society as a result. True incentive pay plans should replace wage type compensation.  Supply and demand for workers in the labor market will also affect wages.

The State and Federal Governments should make it easy to start up a small business as an opportunity for even the poor.  When a new business starts up it should be protected from interferences such as State and Local Government restrictions, regulations requirements and excessive taxes.

Prices of products would come down and quality of products would go up.  It would be easier for people to find jobs.  This would also take people off welfare and unemployment allowing wealth producers to retain more of their wealth.  It would also help relieve the homeless problem.  The individual consumer and the wealth producer would benefit.  The products would be more competitive on foreign markets and help increase exports.

VOTER'S VETO

Each active political party should develop a list of any of past legislation passed by congress that they would like to see rescinded.  These lists would then be delivered to the annual Governor's convention and the Governors would vote up or down on each item to determine if it should be put on the ballot of the next general election for the voters of the nation to vote on as a "voter's veto".  The purpose would be to review all legislation passed by congress and, possibly, state and federal Governments.  This voter's veto would bring the Government closer to the people.

Any important legislation that was undesirable to the society could be placed on the ballot to be voted on by the People in the next general election.  If two thirds majority, for example, voted the legislation undesirable the legislation would be rescinded.  A "voter's veto".  This system should be able to review all legislation in the US, past and future legislation. Give the Government back to the People.

The voters must have a veto power.  We must bring Government closer to the people.  This "voter's veto" would improve any Democracy.  If we do not demand more respect from the Government we will become slaves to our own Government.  Our Government personnel will develop the attitude that they are the "authorities", that they are "supreme", that they are "the honorable", that they are the "officials", that we, the People are merely a source of revenue, that we are their slaves.

172

With our various Governments creating thousands of new laws each year, how can we possibly be becoming a freer People? How often do our various Governments eliminate laws that do not work or that we do not like? Very seldom!

We of the US society cannot possibly be maintaining our freedom when literally thousands of new laws are dumped upon our society each year by the various Governments of the US and none ever eliminated. Even though more of the laws enacted by the various Governments tend to ruin society than benefit society they are almost never removed. We need "Voter's Veto".

The US Government is changing. It is changing from "A Government of the People, by the People, for the People", where all the Government personnel are servants of the People to "A People of the Government, by the Government, for the Government" which is an authoritarian Government. Rather than all Government personnel being servants of the People, "We, the People have become servants of our Government. The switch has been made because "We, the People" have allowed Government to change it.

The US has one of the few Governments in the history of the world where the people can demand that the Government be the government we want it to be through Democracy. But we must demand that our elected servants make our Government conform and perform the way we want. We must insist that our Government personnel be servants of the People or Government will turn us into slaves of the government. We will become slaves of our own Government.

In a Democratic form of Government, politicians and law enforcement personnel are not authorities or superiors or gods. They are servants or leaders of the people. We must not forget that or we may forget the goal of Democracy, which is freedom for the individual. No one in a Democratic form of Government is an authority. They are all servants or leaders of the people.

The Governments of a society will pass legislation from time to time that establishes an agency which does nothing but transfer wealth. The wealth producer or tax payer should have the ability to veto this type of legislation through a voter's veto. The wealth producers of a society have a right to control how their tax money is spent.

When our servants in Government, the politicians vote themselves an excessive pay raise the people should have the ability to take it away with a voter's veto.

173

When our servants take away excessive wealth from the wealth producer through excessive taxes the people should be able to say, "NO NEW TAXES", through a "Voter's Veto".

With a voter's veto, wealth producers would not need unions. They could communicate their demands directly to Government.

When our servants pass laws that pertain to everyone except themselves we should be able to say, "If it does not apply to you politicians, it does not apply to us!" through a voter's veto. A voter's veto would bring the people closer to Government and politicians would have more respect for the individual voter.

We have the technology to set up voting systems across the nation that would not let any one voter duplicate his or her vote. We have the technology to set up a voter's veto.

## WE NEED A NEW POLITICAL PARTY!

We need a new political party! A political party in addition to the Republican and Democrat parties in the US. A party for the entrepreneur, and for opportunity, and against excessive rules and regulations. A political party for the wealth producer and against a welfare state. A political party for the individual and against excessive Government interference and transfer of wealth.

## PARTY PLATFORM

ECONOMY AND BUDGET - Oppose all tax increases, politician's deficit be damned. Support a balanced budget amendment. Support a voter's veto or line item veto. Raise percentage of votes required for Congress to raise taxes or Government pay. Restrict Government hiring. Encourage competition to all entrenched businesses. Promote competition to eliminate monopoly.

DEFENSE - Must retain enough military for sufficient power to maintain security.

WOMEN - Equal rights amendment, freedom of choice, extend equal rights to all jobs and opportunities, public and private.

CHILD CARE - Double present deductions for first two children.

EDUCATION - Merit pay for teachers, back to basics in curriculum, testing of teachers.

DRUGS - Legalize illicit drugs, impose high taxes on those

174

drugs.  Eliminate all prohibition laws.  The drug wars have created a drug industry.

CRIME - Oppose any victimless type laws such as moral standards or prohibition laws.  Pass laws that protect individuals from being victimized.  Allow victims more say in sentencing of criminals.

In a Democratic society the individual must demand respect from the Government.  The individual must demand through voting and special referendums if necessary that all Governments of the society respect the individual.  (See VOTERS VETO - Page 172)  Because with the Government's backing and the Government willing to help, special interests will take everything the wealth producer has, including freedom.  The individual must demand respect from the Government.

If the legislative bodies of a society produce laws that conform to the wills of special interests or groups at the expense of the individual, the individual becomes a slave to the group or special interest.  Compulsory insurance laws may  be an example of the individual becoming a slave to  special interests.

The analytical minds, The independent minds, the creative people, the aggressive, ambitious people, the productive people must unite.  They must demand that their concerns be addressed.  They must unite behind a political party  for the wealth producer.

State Governments watch like vultures as another brave State Government tries a new tax or mandatory money collecting scheme.  If the voter does not complain too much the vultures pass similar legislation.

When a person does finally realize the right to vote, this right to vote is not only a privileged but a responsibility.  All voters have the responsibility to educate themselves in the basics of economics and to know what is good for the economy and what is bad, then to elect people who also have that ability.

For a society to be strong economically, it must require that all able members of a society be productive members.

All legislation should be positive legislation that promotes the productive attitude, legislation that discourages non productive attitude.

THE AUTHORITARIANS ARE COMING

A few hundred years ago people left Europe and came to America to get away from authoritarian rules and regulations that did nothing more than force moral standards upon the individual. These people wrote a constitution and set up a Democratic Government in the hope that the people would protect themselves from such authoritarian rules and regulations.

But these authoritarian prohibitions insist on infiltrating into our society. Prohibitions such as laws against alcohol, flag burning, drugs, pornography, prostitution, gambling merely challenge defiant individuals to rebel against authority. These prohibitions thereby create challenges for defiant individuals to become heroes and martyrs.

The person in prison who has not victimized another individual in society is not a criminal. These prohibitions fill our jails and prisons with non criminals that cost the taxpayers billions.

Trying to control these acts cost the taxpayers billions of dollars each year for law enforcement and confinement and there are no victims. If there are victims, it is the Government's job to protect victims. But it is not the Government's job to harass individuals who are not victimizing anyone. It is absolutely no body's business except the individuals directly involved.

If an individual victimizes him or herself, it is no one's business but his or her own. Government should not try to protect someone from him or herself.

If a society eliminated these prohibition laws, the defiance would not be considered a "macho", "cool" activity by the defiant and their followers. Society should not try to prohibit it.

The Federal Government should rescind, eliminate, do away with all laws, rules, regulations, Federal, Local and State that ban, bar, forbid, prohibit an individual from indulging in personal moral activities that do not victimize other members of the individual's society. Controversial moral issues should never be legislated into law.

One of the major problems of high school students in the US today is alcohol abuse. In many European countries there is no prohibition of alcohol being sold to minors. They do not have the alcohol problems the US has. The high school alcohol problem in the US is another example of defiance and rebellion against authoritarian rule. It is also a form of age discrimination. Let the kids grow up.

Suppose in the case of the flag burning incident the Government, instead of making laws that forbid flag burning, offered the flag burner more flags to burn and suggested that there were more where they came from. This would eliminate the reason for the flag burner to burn flags.

The authoritarian attitude of the Government would be gone. There would be no more reason to be defiant. He would no longer be considered a hero or martyr. The reason any defiant person is considered a martyr is because he or she is brave enough to defy authoritarian rule.

The authoritarian laws forbidding flat burning only create challenges for the defiant and rebellious to burn more flags. No amount of laws can force anyone to be patriotic. In fact excessive laws may cause some people to be less patriotic. Freedom means freedom from excessive laws.

An individual should not be forced to obey rules made up by a group that are intended to be in the best interest of the group, simply for the benefit of the group. This is authoritarian rule.

When rules are made in the best interest of the group they are, in reality, in the best interest of the leader or leaders of the group. The "group" are merely sheep or "groupies" who have been seduced by the leader or leaders to accept and promote the opinions and theories of the leader or leaders. No one knows what is in the best interest of the group. No one is a group but everyone is an individual. Only each individual knows what is in the best interest of him or her.

The group always has a majority over and individual. All groups are made up of individuals. That is why the group should protect the individual.

Government should protect the individual from the infringing, harassing, intimidating pressures of a group. Government should protect the smaller from being victimized by the bigger, the smaller from being taken advantage of by the bigger. That is what the individual pays his taxes to the Government to be protected from. That is US freedom. That is the type of Government the people who wrote the constitution intended to establish and hoped that it would endure. That is the type of protection the wealth producer wants the Government to deliver. Protect the individual from victimization.

When a society goes into the "easy lifestyle" cycle is when the authoritarian attitude develops. The people of the society have less hardships, challenges and risks. And, as a result, less analytical ability is developed. Independent minds become weak minds. The society begins to ask for guidelines and regulations.

Authoritarian figures take advantage of the weak minded groupie, the follower, the sheep, the wealth transfer recipient. When individuals lose their independent minds they become weak and easy to organize into groups. That is where gangs come from, that is where tribes come from. Groups of these people have developed a majority in society because of excessively easy lifestyles. That is where the special interest organizations come from. That is where socialist societies come from.

These groupies feel they need standards to guide them because they do not have the analytical ability to determine for themselves what is right and what is wrong. These are the people that vote into office the authoritarian figures. These are the people who say we need tax increases to create more welfare and subsidies and bigger Government.

Individuals are too independent to organize. That is why individuals usually lose out in a Democracy. And as the individuals lose their mental capabilities due to easy life styles, they join the groupies. The society becomes a socialist society.

Authoritarian rule, through threats, repression, intimidation and fear does effectively reduce crime but the people of the "Arab Spring" countries are saying they would rather have a little more permissiveness and a lot less authoritarian repression, lies, threats and fear.

A person can demand obedience through fear by being deadly. But a person can only earn respect by being fair. People will respect a person and follow him or her as a fair leader but they will fear that person if he or she is deadly (as are some dictators and some authoritarian Governments) or if the person threatens their source of livelihood or freedom. They may follow or hide or bow and obey out of fear.

Some people falsely believe a person with class is a person who has fancy clothes or money or a person who has a powerful position. They believe that those conditions are what makes the person a person with class. They also believe since they are people of class they are better than the rest of society. Some people also believe they are the chosen people because of their religion.

There is a difference between a person with class and a person with no class but it does not have anything to do with money or powerful positions or fancy clothes or genes or family background or religion and it does not make them better than the rest of society.

Class is having character, honesty and consideration for others. Class is having a healthy, shapely body. Anyone can have this type of class.

Some of the people who believe there is a high class and a low class in a society also believe a person is born into a specific class and that a person will die in that same class. They believe that no one can change the class into which a person is born. They also believe that a genius is born a genius. They believe that the genius capabilities are inherited through his or her genes.

Many people use this theory of tremendously influential, inherited genes as an excuse to be lazy bums. They theorize that since they were not born with the genes to become a genius, why even try. Others believe that they were naturally gifted and do not even have to try to maintain their "superiority".

There is no high class or low class in any society! There is no superior or inferior class. There is only one class. It does not matter what nationality, what sex, what color, what religion or what monarchy. All people are born equal. The inherited genes make very little difference. The environment of the individual, after he or she is born, is what makes the difference in people. Everyone has the potential, the brain capacity to be a genius.

Similarly, some religions believe the people of their particular religion are the chosen class and all societies should live by their rules. This is a reason why religion should be separated from Government. The bloodiest wars of the world have been, and still are, religious wars.

Similarly, in the ethnic problems of nationalities and tribes in the world the belief that one nationality or tribe is a class above all others is the basic cause of clashes and conflict. An example is Hitler and the Jews.

The authoritarian figure has a secret that he or she does not want non authoritarian people to know about. The authoritarian believes that people are born with their destiny programmed before them and the authoritarian was born to be the leader, the ruler. The analytical person was born to be his or her servant. The authoritarian is a master at the art of deceit and politics.

Authoritarians do not believe that people have the ability to develop brain power, analytical ability. They believe they are the intelligent class. They tend to be over confident. They believe some people were born to be underclass and some were born to be superior class, the Napoleon Bonaparte attitude. Many people develop this attitude if they are in a powerful position for very long such as politicians. That is why we must have term limits in politics.

179

No one likes authoritarian rule whether it is in a family or a society. When I was very young I saw this happen in a home in which I was living. A child who was still too young to talk began to wake up at night and cry. The child was afraid of an authoritarian parent. When the child would start crying the parent would loudly command the child to be quiet. This would scare the child even more and the child would begin to scream. The parent would then get up and spank the child extremely hard until the child was so afraid that it stopped crying but then gasped for air. This went on for several nights until the child was too afraid to even begin to cry. I was too young and too afraid to express my opinion but I developed a huge dislike for the authoritarian parent.

Sometimes in child abuse cases the parent is frustrated because of the child's screaming. The frustration can cause the parent to become violent enough to kill. But the child is saying, "I would rather die than live in such authoritarian environment". The child is rebelling against authoritarian rule.

People with the authoritarian attitude usually have kids who are belligerent and defiant and addicted to whatever was the passion of the time. The authoritarian's kids did not like authoritarian rule either.

One of the biggest problems in all authoritarian Governments is that the people in power develop the feeling that the wealth created and produced by the people of that society belongs to them, the people in power. Beyond that they feel these people that create and produce the wealth are a tool of the Government and belong to the Government also.

These powerful Government figures develop the feeling, the attitude that they are a class above the wealth producers. And the groupies that follow them worship them like gods. The longer these powerful Government figures remain in power, the stronger that feeling or attitude becomes. If these powerful Government figures were forced by law to return to civilian life after a specific number of years of service the development of that attitude would be interrupted and the society would benefit.

More than in any other occupation, a person in a position of authority such as police or military or Government must be required to pay the full price for any miss deeds or miss use of authority. They should also be required to abide by the same rules and laws that everyone else has to live with. If they are allowed to get away with inhuman acts toward or treatment of the individual then the society is in serious danger of human injustice. It is important that all politicians be required to live by the rules and regulations that they force upon the people of a society. Any legislative body that legislates laws that apply to others but not to them is a dangerous group.

A dictatorship or monarchy could be as good a Government as a Democratic Government except for one problem. Very few individuals can hold a powerful governing position over the people of a society for very long without developing the attitude that he or she is of a class somewhere above or superior to the people of that society. If he or she feels superior that means he or she feels that the people of the society are inferior. This is a false attitude and a Democratic Government is a better Government because (and when) it replaces the members of Government periodically.

All members of a society resent being treated as low class or inferior because they know they are of equal class. The US Constitution was an attempt to make rules so that all people would be treated equally.

Management should never treat employees as inferior. Management should always treat all employees as equals because they are, in fact, equals. Each individual employee is equal to all other employees, including bosses.

An employee can never truthfully be accused of insubordination because he or she is always equal to his or her boss. A boss can never be superior because no one is inferior. The way a boss should earn respect is by being an honest, fair, considerate, worthy leader. A boss can not attempt to be a class above or superior and, for this sole reason, expect to be respected.

But the individual can have character traits that reduce his or her productivity to the point that his or her production is not worth the compensation he or she receives. Character traits such as dishonesty, not being dependable, laziness, interfering with other employees productivity, etc., would be examples. If they are not productive the management should have the right to fire them.

Any employee should have the right to refuse to work in any condition or situation or location that the employee feels in unsafe. And that employee should be protected by Government regulatory agencies from hostile consequences or reprisal by the employer.

# ANALYTICAL MIND

Similar to the muscle and fitness gyms that develop muscle and healthy bodies, our society needs Mental Fitness Gyms to strengthen the mental weaklings of our society. Mental fitness gyms that develop the analytical ability of the brain. The public schools are not doing the job.

The muscle's strength is recognized in its ability to lift a large amount of weight. The brain's strength is recognized in its ability to analyze. Creative thinking and common sense are a result of analyzing. Most of the time formal education uses the ability to remember or memorize, not the ability to analyze. Problem solving and business success require the ability to analyze.

Analytical ability is to the brain as physical strength is to the muscles. If you do not use it, it will disappear. But if you do use it, the more intensely and the more often you use it, the more analytical you will become, the more analytical ability you will have.

The difference in shallow thinking and deep thinking is the difference in concentration. Concentration in thinking is similar to the weights used in weight lifting. The heavier the weights you use in weight lifting the stronger you become. In exercising and strengthening the brain, the deeper or heavier you concentrate while thinking, the more powerful your brain becomes.

Everyone needs analytical ability because analytical ability is essential for protecting our individual freedoms and for the individual planning and problem solving necessary for the production of wealth in a free market.

Talent is nothing more, nor nothing less than analytical ability. Self discipline and hard work contribute to the analytical mind. Laziness is the analytical mind's worst enemy.

You can develop an analytical mind by creating hardships for yourself and then accepting the challenges. You can develop an analytical mind by solving math problems and by solving continuously more difficult math problems. All students should take as much math as possible. Solving math problems is a good way to develop analytical ability. Debate teams are very good for helping to develop analytical minds.

You can develop an analytical mind by taking risks and accepting the challenges and solving the problems that result. You can develop an analytical mind by writing creative material and music, by doing creative art. Playing chess is a good mental challenge.

Hardship causes the people of a society to develop analytical ability. When the rules and laws are made to eliminate hardship the members of society do not have to use their brain power to solve the problems caused by the hardship and the brain loses its analytical ability.

An analytical mind does not accept things exactly as they are presented. Instead, an analytical mind takes things that are expected to be accepted as presented and tears them apart, analyzes them.

Creativity is taking two or more ideas that someone else thought up and combining them to make a new and unique, different idea that solves a given problem.

When the majority of the population in a society has lost its analytical ability, the ability to solve its own problems, it then starts to demand that the Government furnish standards and guidelines. That is when the individuals of the society start to lose their freedoms in the best interest of the group or special interests, sometimes called "common good". That is an invitation for totalitarianism or authoritarianism.

The analytical capabilities of the brain in the US society is going down the tube, the TV tube. TV is simply not a challenge to the brain.

Exercise your brain and you can become as good at learning as anyone, at any age. Because the brain, like the muscles, needs exercise to become stronger and without constant exercise can become weak. Thinking is the exercise that strengthens the brain. TV usually does not challenge a person to think or encourage a person to think or even allow a person to think.

That is why TV is so destructive to analytical ability. It is not a challenge to the brain. And if you were not watching TV you may be reading a book or a newspaper or doing something else that is challenging to the brain.

Of course some reading is no more challenging to the brain than TV, such as comics. But many analytical, thoughtful writers and reporters do write material that gives the brain a challenge. Solving various problems on the job and problems in everyday life can challenge the brain. Hardships challenge the brain. Disabilities, mistakes and accidents and taking risks challenge the brain.

These challenges to the brain are similar to exercise for the muscles. The more often your brain encounters the challenges and solves the problems and the more challenging the challenges become, the more analytical ability the brain develops, giving the brain the ability to solve tougher and tougher problems.

Boredom is a waste of time. But aggressive individuals with analytical minds will not allow themselves to be bored. They will search for challenges and even create challenges both mental and physical.

Hunger and danger are both challenges in nature and wild animals learn to find food and to protect themselves from danger. The alert ones survive and reproduce, one of nature's ways of rewarding alertness and maintaining strength of the species. True free market works similarly, the alert, analytical individual survives the risks, hazards, competition and challenges by being able to solve problems. The reward is success.

Another example of a hardship that an individual can impose upon him or herself is to force him or herself to live for two weeks with only twenty dollars to buy food. Hunger is very stimulating. The brain will begin to produce surprisingly good ideas. The stimulation and challenge can cause creative thinking, almost as stimulating and challenging as going on a two week hike into the wilderness.

When socialism takes away the free market it eliminates self discipline the individual must have to do individual planning, to solve his or her individual problems.

GENIUS

Except in a situation where the brain has reduced capacity due to injury or illness, all people have the brain capacity to become a genius. Genius is created by the brain strenuously working to analyze and overcome hardship and frustration.

The brain is similar to a muscle. When it is used and exercised it becomes more powerful. The brain has tremendous capacity and capabilities and even when injured by illness or disease can still become tremendously analytical when used and exercised. But the brain must continuously be used and exercised or it will lose strength and capability similar to a muscle.

Some people simply give up when challenged. This is no way to exercise the brain. People must recognize stress and hazard as a challenge, as a chance to exercise the brain. People must then use the brain to solve these hazards and stress problems.

Formal education is way over compensated in our society. Formal education does not produce creative minds or common sense. Compared to the stress, risk, frustration and hazards of real life, formal education is very boring and does not stimulate the brain enough to produce creative minds and common sense. The brain, struggling and strenuously working to solve real life problems caused by stress, risk, frustration, challenges and hardship develops creative minds and common sense. Analytical ability, creative ability and common sense are not developed in formal schooling, they are developed in the school of hard knocks.

Common sense is more valuable than formal education in the management basics of any business. Common sense is the ability to simplify, the ability to recognize the real, true cause of a problem.

A person who has common sense is a person who consistently searches for the truth. A person who does not lie to him or herself. In solving a problem, the individual searches for the real cause of the problem. Even if it means the individual must criticize him or herself as opposed to making excuses for him or herself. It does not matter so much whether a person lies to others. But it is very important that a person does not lie to him or herself.

Sometimes the truth is very hard to detect. But the individual must constantly search for the truth and develop the ability to recognize the truth.

No one is born with common sense. An individual develops common sense by having the guts to accept challenge, to take a risk and then correcting his or her own mistakes as he or she labors through the challenging experience. As the experience becomes more and more challenging the brain is increasingly stimulated and must work harder increasing its analytical and creative ability.

The brain has tremendous capacity. No one ever develops the total potential of his or her brain. Creative people create ideas. What is the value of ideas in a society? A theory is merely an idea. It is not a fact. But it has the potential to become a fact. And over a period of time, as numerous attempts to prove it wrong, fail, it can become a fact.

It is possible for an individual to impose handicaps and hardships upon him or herself in order to develop self discipline and self control. It is also possible, through this process of forcing hardships and handicaps upon him or herself, and then through the self discipline and thought processes required to overcome these hardships and handicaps, an individual can improve his or her creative capabilities and IQ to a point where the individual can become a genius.

You could become a genius or end up somewhere on the way up to that level depending on the amount of sweat an effort you apply and frustration and hardship you endure.


## HANDICAPPED

I do not believe the poor want sympathy. I do not believe the minority groups want sympathy. I do not believe the handicapped want subsidies or sympathy. I believe they want opportunity just like everyone else. And most handicapped are very capable of taking advantage of opportunity, probably more so than people without handicaps. The handicapped have built in hardships that cause them to be extra creative, analytical and brilliant. They have the ability to be very productive. Society should adjust for their comfort and convenience but most of them are not totally helpless. Many handicapped are much more productive than people who are not handicapped.

When we think of the handicapped we usually think of someone who has lost a body part or a body function. Or we think of someone who has a problem that is beyond his or her control. But someone who has allowed him or herself to develop bad habits and then does not have the will power or self discipline or self control needed to get rid of that bad habit is also handicapped. Such as someone who has allowed him or herself to develop bad eating habits and has become obese, or someone who has a drinking or smoking habit.

Some people even force hardships or handicaps upon themselves such as runners or weight lifters or even students. Suppose a runner forces him or herself to run five miles a day. The runner forces this hardship or handicap upon him or herself in order to develop a stronger, healthier, better looking body.

The student can force hardships upon him or herself in order to develop intelligence and analytical ability. But in the process the student and the  runner are also developing self discipline and self control.

It does not matter if it is a handicap that is beyond the individual's control or a handicap caused by a bad habit or a handicap the individual forced upon him or herself, everyone has handicaps. When a businessman  runs out of credit he has a handicap. The important thing is whether the individual gives up and allows the handicap to control his or  her life or whether the individual, through self discipline and pure hard effort or hard work, overcomes the handicap. Laziness is self discipline's worst enemy.

The more severe the handicap, the more self discipline and self control the individual must develop in order to overcome the handicap. No one is born with self discipline or self control. The more severe the handicap is and the more self discipline the individual uses to overcome the handicap the stronger the individual's character becomes. Also, as the individual uses more self discipline and self control to solve the problems and to overcome the handicap the individual develops self confidence and analytical ability. Also the individual begins to overcome laziness.

SELF DISCIPLINE

Self discipline is self control not self punishment. You can not punish yourself and like yourself at the same time. Punishment is almost always negative. In this book discipline does not mean punishment. Discipline means control.

An individual needs self discipline and self control in order to develop and keep habits that the body and the mind need and to eliminate habits that are not needed.

You can have self discipline in one thing such as aerobics or eating habits. But as you begin to understand self discipline you can develop self discipline to control your habits in anything you want to attempt. An important first step is to discipline yourself to use and understand self discipline.

If you really want to do something. If you really want to accomplish a goal there are usually several ways to do it. The more creative you are the more ways you can think of. But if you decide not to complete a goal, if you decide to give up, one excuse is usually all that you need.

You can make yourself feel depressed simply by thinking depressing thoughts. But you can also make yourself feel good simply by making yourself think good thoughts. You can control your attitude and moods simply by controlling what you allow yourself to think about, self discipline.

You should repeat to yourself, "I am going to control everything I do. The things I do are not going to control me. I'm going to get my fair share out of this world and I will not let anyone discourage me". But go after your fair share honestly so you can be proud of yourself.

Always build on your character. Never give up. If someone makes upsetting remarks, do not let it interfere. Do not let it cause you to feel sorry for yourself. Feeling sorry for yourself will hurt no one but you. Your character and your future are too important to let mediocre remarks interfere.

Even if a parent says things that hurt your feelings or cause you to lose confidence in yourself, do not let their remarks interfere with your building of character. Do not give up! Because long after you have left home you will still have to live with yourself.

If someone's attitude or irritating ways tend to get the best of you, be persistent! Let it stimulate you. Accept the challenge and push yourself to excel.

Number one, an individual can never give up. No matter what happens, an individual must keep him or herself moving along, trudging along, plodding along. Every trauma, every hardship, every set back is building strength in the brain, brain power, analytical ability, building character. The brain is like a muscle, the strength must be built up slowly.

The difference between a winner and a loser. The winner goes for what he or she wants no matter how hard it is. And the harder it is, the more work it takes to achieve, the more a winner the person becomes. The loser does not care what he or she attempts as long as it is easy.

Laziness is self discipline's worst enemy. Laziness contributes to the lack of analytical ability in society. Laziness is usually the reason for not achieving goals. An "easy living" life style such as we have in our society makes it very difficult not to be lazy.

No one is successful without self discipline. Self discipline takes much effort. It is very difficult to have self discipline and be lazy at the same time.

The difference between society's winners and society's losers. When a winner meets another winner he or she begins, with hard work and sweat, to improve his or her ability until he or she is better than the opponent.

When a loser sees an winner he or she usually makes up and spreads stories and lies about the winner, trying to bring the winner down to his or her level. The loser has allowed laziness to prevent him or her from becoming a winner. The loser has given up. A winner never quits, a quitter never wins.

As long as you keep building up your self discipline and self control you can keep making your goals more and more difficult until you have built yourself into a winner. Anyone can do this. After you have built yourself into a winner you will find that you like yourself a lot more and that you are more confident.

No one accepts a challenge and wins in the first attempt. If the person wins with the first attempt it was not a challenge. It was too easy.

Do not give yourself an ultimatum or a deadline. Especially if you are already having difficulties with your confidence. If you miss a deadline you will hate yourself even more. Just keep plugging on until you achieve.

If you want to change a habit or start a new habit or eliminate and old habit you must be persistent. If you blow it, start over. (Most people cannot change a habit by changing it one time. If they can, they already have self discipline.) You cannot stop smoking by quitting one time or you cannot lose weight by changing your eating activities one single time. It is not that simple. Even ten times will not be enough. You must be persistent. You must have self discipline. You must have will power. You must have determination. You must have stamina. You must be committed. You will attempt to change a habit many times. Maybe a hundred times or more. But each time you continue to work on that habit you will be developing those characteristics listed above. And by the time you have attempted to change that habit many times you will have developed several of those characteristics and you possibly will also have succeeded in changing the habit.

## LAST DEBATE BETWEEN ROMNEY AND OBAMA

I watched the last debate between Mr. Romney and Mr. Obama October 22. 2012. Mr. Romney said he wanted to get private investment to create new jobs again.

In his rebuttal, Mr. Obama said "Private investment does not work. It never did." That was a huge statement! What does he think caused the United States to be the most productive country in the history of the world in the past 100 years? What caused all that wealth to be created? It definitely was not "Government investment". That fits nicely with his statement, "You didn't build that". Do all Keynesians believe that? Do all socialists believe that? Do all Democrats believe that?

All Government spending is tax revenue created by the private investment and private wealth production. The only thing that improves any economy is wealth creation through private investment and workers in private enterprise producing wealth. That is why cutting deficits and cutting Government spending does not hurt an economy, it helps an economy.

All socialist countries are desperate. All socialist countries are desperate because sooner or later they always run out of other people's money. The wealth producers get tired of being the sucker and quit producing wealth. It takes problem solving analytical ability to be a leader. Socialists are not leaders, they are destroyers. Are socialists afraid of reality or is it that they don't have the analytical ability to recognize reality?

# A FEW CLOSING THOUGHTS

## MUTILATING THE WORD "FAIR"

It appears to me Democrats are very abusive to the word "fair". What I would call fair is if workers were allowed to retain more of the wealth they produce rather than having it taxed away to pay for entitlements, or forced through mandates to pay for some other person's health care or car repair or profits. If Democrats worked harder to get their voters to get a job, they would not have to work so hard to mutilate the word "fair".

## ENTITLEMENTS

Entitlements such as they are called by the people who create and promote entitlements are not really entitlements. The promoters and creators of subsidies to the lazy and less fortunate want them to sound legitimate so they call them entitlements. As in the word, "fair", they are mutilating the word entitlements   The entitlement recipients are not necessarily "entitled" to them.

## LIES

Another word mutilated by some people is the word "lies". Some people accuse another person of "lies" by totally distorting the information the other person presents, And some people deny "lies" about some of their information that is totally unreal and untrue.


## THOUGHT MAKES PEOPLE WISE

Irritation, challenges and hazards make people think. Thought makes people wise. And wise people are the winners.

## RELIGION AND SEXUAL ACTIVITY

Christianity and especially Catholicism do more to cause homosexuality than any other social activity in the world. Abstinence and celibacy are the causes because sex is a natural desire and you cannot suppress it or eliminate it. You only divert it into perversion.

## ECONOMICS

Economics is about the storing and production of wealth for survival. Economics is the study and practice of all techniques of survival of all humans.

## CITY BLIGHT

Politicians wonder why there is blight in their city. Excessive taxes and excessive regulations are the main causes of city blight. It should be obvious to any politician who really wants to know, who really wants to be realistic. The endless processing times to get permits and licenses required. The requirements for bonds, surveys, licenses, fees, taxes, the zoning laws, insurance. With all these requirements, regulations and restrictions, it should be obvious why there is blight in their city.

Many of these requirements are kept relatively secret until a future business owner applies for a business license. Then he is hit with the big surprise. A very frustrating experience for anyone.

Politicians keep adding legislation on top of legislation, never removing laws that do not work. And it is amazing how politicians seem to believe that adding onto these laws is the way to get rid of blight in their city.


Osama bin Laden once said, "when people see a strong horse and a weak horse, by nature they will like the strong horse". The US must always be the strong horse. Nobody likes a weak horse.

We don't always have to have a winner or loser. We can each have our own opinion. That is called freedom.

No one should look for blame or fault or feel sorry for themselves. Everyone should look for reality.

THE QUESTION IS; will the spending and the bailouts the Government has been distributing recently produce more wealth than the amount spent? If it does it will be beneficial for the economy. But if the Government's recent spending produces less wealth in the economy than the amount spent, then the spending was a waste and the economy will still improve in spite of the spending but the wasted wealth will be a drag on the economy.

## WHO IS A WEALTH PRODUCER?

There was an article in a news paper that asked, "what do musicians produce? Is their music wealth?" If the music affects the society's wealth producers in a positive way, then the music helps produce wealth.

If Government workers or any workers in the Service Industry help wealth producers produce even more wealth, then the workers are also wealth producers.

Government, digging holes and filling them back in or building bridges to nowhere or spending money that does not produce wealth are examples of destruction of wealth.

## WHAT IS WEALTH?

Wealth is anything that has enough demand from consumers that a price can be put on it. Anything that consumers are willing to pay for.

It doesn't matter if you are a socialist, a capitalist or somewhere in between. A human society must have a wealth producing economy in order to survive.

## FREE MARKET

A free market is a market with a minimum of taxes and regulations and a maximum of freedom to compete and freedom to pursue opportunity. For maximum wealth production, regulations should not interfere with incentives to produce wealth.

## WHY THE UNEMPLOYMENT RATE IS GOING DOWN

The unemployment rate is going down in 2011 because the Government's unemployment compensation is coming to an end. The unemployed realize that if they cannot get unemployment money they will have to get a job. If the Government extends the unemployment compensation, the unemployment rate will go back up.

## LEADERS

What do we want in a leader? Someone who has their brain plugged in. If you want to unplug your brain and let someone else do your thinking for you, vote for a Democrat.

## COMPETITION IS THE BEST REGULATION EVER INVENTED

Competition is a natural regulator of the free market.

## MISTAKES ARE THE MOST PRODUCTIVE EDUCATIONAL TOOL EVER INVENTED

If people were forced to learn from their mistakes as opposed to being forced to buy insurance, the people of the society would be much more responsible, respectful, competent, successful, prudent, analytical, healthy and hard working and more intelligent. The economy would be much improved.

Mistakes are as important as successes. People learn much more from their mistakes than their successes. Mistakes are the most productive educational tools ever invented. If the Government does not allow people to learn the full lesson from their mistakes, the whole society suffers.

I would love to see people healthier, happier, wealthier and more intelligent.

## THE PROBLEM WITH GOVERNMENT INVESTING

The difference between Government investing and private investing is that when the private investor makes a mistake, he or she suffers the consequences. When the Government makes an investment mistake, the tax payers suffer the consequences. The Government should never make investments.

## WHAT SHOULD POLITICIANS AND REGULATORS DO TO

STIMULATE A WEAK ECONOMY? NOTHING! STAY OUT OF THE WAY!

## DEMOCRACIES SELF DESTRUCT
As democracies age they tend to self destruct because they add on new taxes and regulations on top of the old taxes and regulations. They never eliminate old taxes or regulations. The constipation destroys entrepreneurship, opportunity, free market and wealth production.

## CONTROLLING MEDICAL COSTS
The only way to control medical costs is to switch the goal of searching for medical cures by corporations to searching for causes of illnesses. They only want to find cures. They do not want people to know the cause. If people eliminate the cause they won't make any money.

## MAXIMUM PRODUCTIVITY - INCENTIVE
In capitalism, incentive has much more potential value than society realizes. If the payment system used to pay for work produced was changed from a wage paying system to a fair and aggressive incentive pay system a capitalist economy would produce much more wealth. Everyone would be better off, even the owners.

## U.S. CRITICISM OF OTHER COUNTRIES
Accusing any country of manipulating its currency is misguided. It is any country's sovereign right to control its currency. The US manipulates its currency as much as any country, and more than most.

When the US is manipulating its currency downward in order to help corporations export more it is irritating and embarrassing to hear US regulators and politicians accuse other countries of manipulating their currencies. The whole world can see what is going on. So who is the ignorant one?

## MARKET MAKING
Banks and brokers should not be allowed to be involved in market making activities. Bankers and brokers are extremely bias in favor of themselves and as a result against investors.

BUYING CHINESE IMPORTS

We buy Chinese imports and then China loans us our money back so we can buy more Chinese stuff.

That's like the farmer who sold all his horses to his neighbor. But he still had some hay left. Not to worry because the neighbor loaned him back the horses so they could eat up all the hay.


The Government should keep all regulations simple enough so that they can explain what the regulation is intended to do. If they cannot explain what the regulation is intended to do, they should not pass the regulation. And if the regulation doesn't work as intended, it should be immediately eliminated.

ABOUT END OF LIFE COUNCELING AND DEATH SQUADS.

The politicians say that if end of life counseling is passed there will be no death squads. But the politicians are not going to be the ones making the final decisions. The people on the ground are. And the reality is, some form of premature deaths are going to happen (they already are) and the politicians won't do anything about them.

IS THERE ONLY ONE GOD FOR ALL RELIGIONS?

I saw a headline in a news paper; "Is there only one God for all religions"? That is a very good question. But I have other questions. "Is there NO Super Human God for any religion"? Is God a fantasy? Are the only rules we have, natures rules?

Are all the Gods of various religions going to have a war in the heavens and start throwing stars at each other?

Is religion anything more than negative theories? If it feels good don't do it. If it tastes good spit it out.

THE EXCUSE OF GENES

I can't do that. It's not in my genes.

Too many people use some type of gene theory as an excuse to be lazy. I don't care if my combination of genes is the lowest in the world, I will never allow any gene theory to stop me from accomplishing what I want to accomplish. I don't even want to know what that theory is.

All the theories about genes being the problem or cause should be listed in the category of "old wives tales". Gene theories are used as an excuse to defend human failures. That is all they are, excuses.

## SOCIALISM
Rules for the good of everyone and for the satisfaction of none, called "common good".

Let's see there is a million, billion, trillion. What comes after trillion? At the rate Government is printing phony money we are going to be there very shortly.

Don't let fear of making a mistake keep you from trying. You learn a lot more from your mistakes than your successes.

LIBERAL - The term liberal was derived from politicians with the attitude that they should solve all society's problems by throwing other people's money at those problems. In other words be liberal with other people's money.

## CREDIT CAN NOT BE GIVEN! CREDIT MUST BE EARNED!
You should not have credit if you cannot pay it back.

## STAGFLATION
Excessive liquidity also caused the stagflation that we had in the late 1970's. Stagflation happens when financial institutions find they can make more money by being involved in intrusive Government programs than they can through private investing.

## BALANCE, FAIRNESS AND SHARED RESPONSIBILITY
Democrats say the Republican budget "does not stand the test of balance, fairness and shared responsibility". But the Democrats want to use taxpayer money to give out subsidies, handouts and bail outs to everyone. That's not balance, fairness and responsibility, that's welfare.
What is fair? Turning the wealth producers into slaves for the welfare recipients, the subsidized, the Government employees, the lazy, the entitlement seekers? Is that what Democrats call fair? Is that what Democrats call balanced? Is that what the Democrats call shared responsibility?

Government should not slow the cost of living increases of social security. Inflation is not the senior citizen's fault. It is 100% the Government's fault. Social security is a true entitlement the seniors deserve because they paid for it. Many senior citizens will never get back in social security payments what they and their bosses paid in.

Wealth producers paid in some form of profit sharing or incentive pay or independent contracting rather than hourly wages would produce much more wealth. The creative individuals would excel.

Team work groups are like a chain. They are as strong as their weakest link. The strongest producers are held back by the weakest producers. The ambitious become bored and leave.

The services sector produces much less real wealth in the economy than the industrial sector. For that reason the services sector burns more wealth than it creates. Some of the services are more of a drag on the economy than a benefit. In hard times, you can't eat services, you can't wear services, services don't keep you warm or sheltered. In other words they are not necessary for basic survival.

If Keynesians believe they can print all the money they need to get themselves out of trouble, why do they even bother to collect taxes? Why don't they just print all the money the Government needs and let the people keep their money?

The reason why the Government has to collect taxes is because the Government has no choice. Money must be backed up by real wealth created by wealth producers. Government cannot just print money at its convenience without destroying the currency and the economy. That is why in years past, money was backed up by gold and silver. Back then, Government economists had problem solving abilities.

On November 22, 2012, Mr. Bernanke said he wants to keep the expansionary and low interest rate stimulus policies going even after the economy improves. That means he plans to continue destroying the currency. Destroying the currency is exactly what is causing the weakness in the economy. That is what Japan has been doing for the past twenty years. Do we want to have a long term, weak "Japanese" type economy like we have had for the past five years?

Mr. Obama said in 2012 that he would mow Mr. Boehner's or Mr. McConnell's lawn or polish their shoes in order to fix the fiscal cliff. Then he turns around and says that he won't sign anything for less than a 1.6 trillion dollar tax increase. I didn't realize the dollar had lost that much value during his last term. Talk about inflation! That means the dollar is absolutely worthless.

"Other people's money" is your and my tax dollars. We are the slaves that produce the confiscated wealth.

Socialism is nothing more than a vote buying scandal buying votes with other people's money.

# TABLE OF CONTENTS

www.ingramcontent.com/pod-product-compliance
Lightning Source LLC
Chambersburg PA
CBHW051826090426
42736CB00011B/1667